Lost Auburn

LOST AUBURN

A Village Remembered in Period Photographs

Ralph Draughon, Jr.
Delos Hughes
Ann Pearson

NewSouth Books
Montgomery

NewSouth Books
105 S. Court Street
Montgomery, AL 36104

Copyright © 2012 by Ralph Draughon Jr., Delos Hughes, and Ann Pearson.
All rights reserved under International and Pan-American Copyright Conventions. Published in the
United States by NewSouth Books, a division of NewSouth, Inc., Montgomery, Alabama.

Library of Congress Cataloging-in-Publication Data

Draughon, Ralph B. (Ralph Brown)
Lost Auburn : a village remembered in period photographs
/ Ralph Draughon, Jr., Delos Hughes, Ann Pearson.

pages cm

Includes index.

ISBN 978-1-60306-119-3 (trade cloth)
ISBN 978-1-58838-492-8 (trade paper)

1. Auburn (Ala.)—History—Pictorial works. 2. Auburn (Ala.)—Buildings, structures, etc.—Pictorial works. 3. Lost architecture—Alabama—Auburn—Pictorial works. 4. Historic buildings—Alabama—Auburn—Pictorial works. 5. Auburn (Ala.)—Biography.
I. Hughes, Delos D. II. Pearson, Ann B. (Ann Bowling), 1941– III. Title.
F334.A83D73 2012
976.1'55—dc23

2012037344

Design by Randall Williams

Contents

Preface / VII

Acknowledgments / IX

1 The Setting / 3

2 The College / 7

3 A Town of Schools / 47

4 Churches / 61

5 Early Period Houses / 77

6 From the Civil War to World Conflict, 1865–1918 / 91

7 Scrapbook of the Late 19th and Early 20th Centuries / 105

8 Auburn Houses After World War I / 111

9 Businesses / 127

10 Movie Theaters / 143

11 Another Entertaining Business / 151

12 Public Buildings / 155

13 Transportation / 159

14 Peroration / 165

Index / 166

Preface

A newcomer to Auburn can ask nearly anyone on the street what the town is like and be regaled with accounts of the latest housing development or business or park. Former Auburnites, however, returning after some absence, are just as likely to be met with puzzled stares if they ask about parts of the streetscape that are remembered but no longer to be found. The authors of this book are such returnees, coming home after absences of various lengths and more or less infrequent visits while living elsewhere. They believe some record should be compiled of Auburn structures that one can no longer see—buildings that have been destroyed, or so altered as to be no longer recognizable, or that have simply fallen into ruin. That is what we have assembled in the pages that follow—a record of lost Auburn buildings. It is not, of course, a complete record. Much of the original Auburn was lost before photographs were common, and many of the photographs taken years ago, like their subjects, are themselves lost. When we are able to find other records of these buildings, we have included the descriptions and anecdotes that preserve their contributions to Auburn life. In bringing this beginning collection to public attention, we hope more of what is now unknown may come to light, to be included, perhaps, in some future edition.

Marcel Proust famously argued that taste and smell evoked better than pictures the essence of recollection, but we cannot offer our readers the taste of a cup of coffee at the Auburn Grille or a whiff of Pauline Wilkins's pastries at her bakery across the street. It would be even more difficult to describe, much less duplicate, the taste of a banana split at Markle's Drug Store, a shake at The Flush, or a brew at Pop Raines's Beverage Shack. Furthermore, we do not wish to celebrate one pervasive smell of yesteryear that everyone of a certain age can recall: the enveloping presence of cigarette smoke. How did we stand it? Why did we put up with it?

But why try to evoke the past at all? One answer, quite reactionary, might be appropriate to residents of a town that Oliver Goldsmith, at least, indirectly, named. In Goldsmith's play, *She Stoops to Conquer*, Mr. Hardcastle declares, "I love everything that's old: old friends, old times, old manners, old books, old wines." And to that backward-looking declaration, some residents of Auburn would add, very emphatically: "old buildings!"

College students at Auburn in years past, however, might turn to this volume in search, not of everything old, but just the opposite. They might seek to recapture, in essence, their lost youth among the mementos of basketball games at the Barn, movies at the Tiger or the War Eagle, parties at some fraternity house, or socializing at the Casino. And surely that counts as one legitimate purpose of this volume.

This volume was put together in 2011, the 175th anniversary of the town's founding and a year memorable for a national football championship and the poisoning of the ancient live oaks at the main gate of the college at Toomer's Corner. Oddly enough, the legal controversy over the poisoning illustrates sharply contrasting points of view in regard to historic preservation. It epitomizes, aptly, the never-ending debate between the importance of a historic landmark and its very mundane worth as real estate. The alleged perpetrator of the poisoning has faced a battery of charges, including attempting to destroy "a venerable object." On the other hand, his legal defense has argued that according to the Code of Alabama, an oak tree only has the value of $20, and its destruction only meets the criteria of a misdemeanor. At the time of publication, the case had not yet come to trial, and so the legal question remained unresolved.

In a larger sense, the value of Auburn's historic landmarks remains unresolved, as well. But how refreshing to know that at least one "venerable object" in town has invoked legal protection! Alas! This volume identifies many other venerable objects, such as the Drake-Samford House and the original Victorian interior of Samford Hall, that have, most unhappily, been obliterated. Hallowed by tradition, the live oaks at Toomer's Corner remind us of how precious, and how ephemeral, landmarks in our community can be. Must we lose them to appreciate their worth?

Acknowledgments

This collection of Auburn-iana is a collaboration among many more contributors than the three principal authors. On hearing of the project, friends, acquaintances and strangers have contributed treasured family photographs and barely remembered snapshots. Some of these photographs are already familiar to the public, having been previously published in *Auburn: A Pictorial History* by Mickey Logue and Jack Simms, as well as in various Auburn University publications.

In addition, we are indebted to a number of others whose assistance has been crucial to our bringing this volume to press. We are indebted to the staff of the Archives and Special Collections division of the university library, especially to Joyce Hicks, an indefatigable archivist, who lent her ingenuity, tenacity and patience to so many of our searches that we acknowledge her efforts as the sine qua non of this volume. The Alabama Historical Commission, in particular Bob Gamble, was another indispensable contributor to our project.

We are also grateful to the many hands who made our work light. Without their assistance, this book would have remained merely a fond hope of its authors and never have made its way through the many steps that led finally to its publication. In addition to our friends at NewSouth Books, we are greatly indebted to and here acknowledge the following contributors, not all of whom may be aware of having helped us.

Individual Contributors: Ward Allen, Richard Bentley, Margaret Goodman Brinkley, Dixie Conner, Marcia Sugg Coombs, Dwayne Cox, Nathaniel Curtis Jr., Christine Blackburn Danner, Hartwell Davis, William Dean, William L. Dennis, Bob Duncan, Jeri Allen Earnest, Linda Ensminger, Totsie Farr, Ada Wright Folmar, Nancy Young and Robert Fortner, Tommy W. Gordon, Harvey Gosser, Ann Tamblyn Gregory, Margaret Toomer Hall, Joseph Hare Jr., Joanna Hoit, Luther M. Holt, Beth Carlovitz Holtam, Barbara Berman Kamph, John Kemph, Jacque

Kochak, Jay Lamar, Gail Langley, Fran Marshall Libbe, Lan Lipscomb, Julie Wright Littlejohn, Mickey Logue, Mary Lou Matthews, Rennie McLeod, Elsie Foster Mitchell, Carolyn Seagraves Neal, Mary Norman, Ernestine Robinson, Fran Rollins, Linda Tamplin Sanders, Desmond L. Scaife, Katherine Sherrer, Linda Silavent, Jack Simms, Mary Lou Edwards Smith, Emily Amason Sparrow, Henry Stern, Dr. and Mrs. William Sugg Jr., Jessie and Carl Summers, Carolyn and Billy Tamblyn, Virginia Taylor, Beverley Burkhardt Thomas, Jim Whatley, Edward White, Ethell White, Betty Grimes Williams, Rena Williams, Emil Wright, and Bob Yerkey.

Institutional Contributors: Alabama Department of Archives and History, Auburn Church of Christ, Auburn Public Library, Auburn United Methodist Church, Auburn University Library and Archives, Environmental Data Resources Inc., First Baptist Church of Auburn, First Presbyterian Church of Auburn, Holy Trinity Episcopal Church, Lakeview Baptist Church, Lee County Historical Society, Library of Congress, St. Michael the Archangel Catholic Church, and Village Christian Church.

Lost Auburn

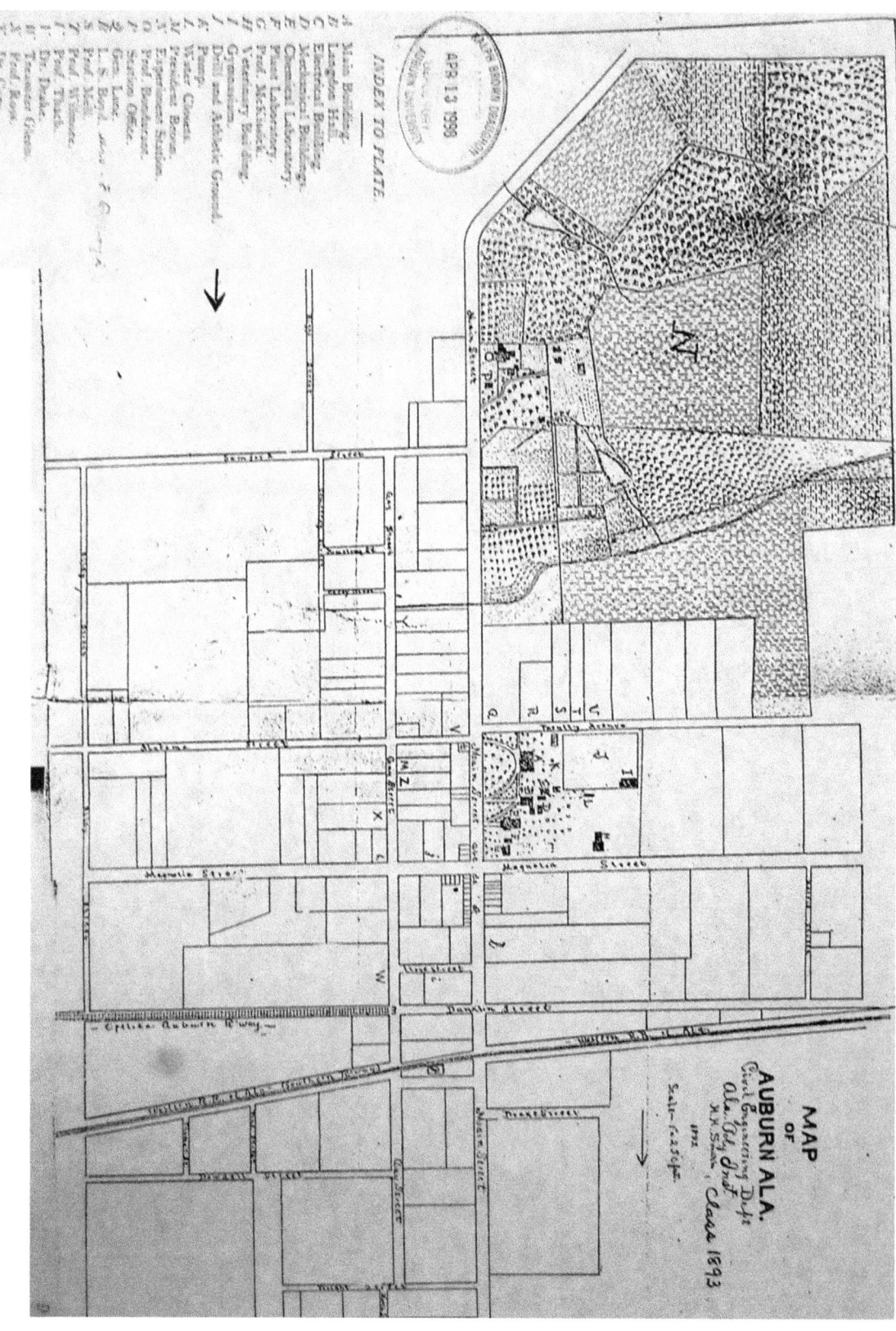

1

The Setting

Today's city takes its name from an eighteenth-century poem by Oliver Goldsmith that celebrated "Auburn, sweet Auburn! Loveliest village of the plain!" The name suited the new community very well, except that the village was situated just inside the Piedmont and not quite on the plains. Auburn indeed was a village, and it remained one well into the twentieth century, as photographs in this volume indicate. Furthermore, early visitors testified to its attractiveness; they remarked on Auburn's ancient shade trees, natural springs, clean air, healthy locale, and neatly maintained houses and gardens. Nevertheless, the village was not situated in a rich agricultural region. When William LeRoy Broun, the late-nineteenth-century president of the college, was asked why the institution had been located in Auburn, he replied with a bit of irony, "For its healthfulness of climate and poverty of soil: any experiment succeeding here would succeed anywhere in the State."

From its earliest days, the village had a difficult to define quality. It possessed character. Besides character, it also had in abundance a supply of characters who certainly added to the community what is known as local color.

The founder of Auburn was Judge John J. Harper of Harris County, Georgia. He led a group of settlers here in late 1836, soon after the forcible removal from east Alabama of the last Native Americans, remnants of the Creek nation. Judge Harper's party included his mother, half-brothers, eleven children, in-laws, their in-laws, his fifty-three slaves, a contingent of other slaves, and assorted livestock.

Most of them were Methodists. Indeed, Judge Harper was the Moses of the Auburn Methodist Church. He led this group of chosen people out of the land of Georgia into a new "Promised Land" where Methodist principles, like temperance, were supposed to be practiced, but where John Wesley's opposition to slavery was paid little heed. Though other denominations soon followed, the Methodists had an important influence on the early history of the village, particularly in outlawing the sale of alcohol and establishing educational institutions.

Judge Harper's half-brother, Nathaniel Scott, led the movement to establish the Auburn Masonic Female College, which opened in 1853, and Scott and the Reverend John Bowles Glenn encouraged the local congregation to establish the East Alabama Male College, a Methodist institution that began classes in 1859 and served as the forerunner of Auburn University.

The first settlers of Auburn met many challenges. They arrived in late 1836, survived the winter, and then encountered the Panic of 1837, a worldwide depression that severely affected Southern agriculture and lasted well into the 1840s. Not surprisingly, then, the pioneering community of Auburn began as a log village of houses and churches. However, the depression ended at last and, beginning in the late 1840s, the village enjoyed unusual prosperity until the Civil War began in 1861.

During the conflict, a blockade of Southern ports imposed severe privation on the community. Federal troops twice raided the village to destroy the railroad that served as a lifeline for the Confederate defense of Atlanta. In the summer of 1864, General Lovell Rousseau and 2,500 Federal cavalrymen tore up thirty-five miles of tracks leading to and from the village, disabled the rolling stock, and burned the depot, the post office and a large warehouse. Local slaves then joined the soldiers in looting the business district. Federal troops made a particular point of looting Pebble Hill, rented by Mrs. William Lowndes Yancey, the widow of the Fire-Eater politician who had done so much to bring about the secession of the Southern states. Although Rousseau's horsemen did not damage local homes, a fierce tornado ripped through the community on December 27, 1864, destroyed houses, and killed five residents. The villagers regarded it a miracle that more were not killed. When the roof of the Baptist Church caved in, the high-backed pews protected the Confederate soldiers who were convalescing in the Gilmer hospital located there. (Sophie Gilmer Bibb of Montgomery organized the Hospital Association to treat wounded Confederates. Perhaps her prominent family subsidized the hospital in the church.)

Federal General James H. Wilson's troops, several thousands in number, raided Auburn at the end of the Civil War and encamped overnight at the spring behind Pebble Hill. Although Wilson's Raiders' stay was brief, they took time to tear up the railroad once more and, this time, to loot private homes as well as businesses.

The Civil War devastated Auburn, leaving the community and the college destitute, and local commerce and staple crop agriculture in ruins with no source of credit to provide funds to start over. The state took over the impoverished Methodist college in 1872, but for many years provided no annual appropriations to run it. By 1888, however, the college and the town showed a few signs of returning prosperity. In that year, a Tuskegee newspaper reported that in the last twelve months, twenty new residences had been built in Auburn. Furthermore, each house cost at least $1,500, and some even cost $5,000.

Fire destroyed individual structures from time to time. According to Tuskegee newspapers, when a fire destroyed the carriage factory on the east side of Main (today's College) Street in 1852, the villagers suspected arson by white workers who resented having to compete with slave labor. The blaze spread quickly along Main Street and was stopped to the north when John G. W. Whale agreed to blow up his doctor's office. To the south, volunteers managed to arrest the fire before it reached "the beautiful business corner" today occupied by Toomer's Drugs.

Simeon Perry's mansion, which cost $25,000 to build, burned in 1859; William F. Samford's Cedre Villa, built by Judge Harper, went up in flames in 1863; and fire consumed James F. Dowdell's house outside Auburn in 1870. In 1893, another fire threatened the mostly uninsured business district. It destroyed five structures before a rainstorm extinguished the flames. Sad to say, however, the house of "Gatsy" Rice, a popular African American seamstress (who later was buried in Pine Hill Cemetery) lost her home and business in the blaze.

By 1907, the enrollment at the college reached 600, which made it at the time the largest student body in Alabama. For some years thereafter housing proved to be a continuing problem for both students and faculty.

The situation improved in 1922, when, according to a Columbus newspaper, residents built fifty-one new homes in Auburn. The newspaper particularly noted that Sheldon Toomer had begun building on West Magnolia the fine Tudor house that Frank Lockwood, the prominent Montgomery architect, designed for him.

The Great Depression of 1929 lasted for more than a decade in Auburn, but New Deal programs contributed importantly to the construction of new buildings on campus. Warren, Knight, and Davis, a Birmingham architectural firm with longstanding ties to the college, designed almost all of the new structures.

Auburn's population tripled from 1940 to 1950. World War II imposed on the community a new housing shortage, but it was dwarfed in scale by the vast post-war enrollment at the college. The G. I. Bill of Rights, which provided a collegiate education for returning veterans, swelled the size of the college and the community and transformed the village into a crowded town. Perhaps the most memorable symbols of the housing shortage were the rows and rows of military surplus "pre-fab" apartments for married students and faculty, and the U.S. Navy surplus deck-houses, for male students (both of which are illustrated in this book).

In 1953, a second tornado struck Auburn. Although of equal severity to the storm that struck during the Civil War, this time no lives were lost. Nevertheless, the storm assaulted two houses important in local history: the Simeon Perry house, which it destroyed, and the Ogletree-Wright-Ivey house, which lost its second story. The tornado also did severe damage to Cary Woods, one of the city's most upscale and popular neighborhoods. No homes were lost, yet the storm toppled a stand of extraordinarily tall and handsome pine trees that had been a distinctive feature of the neighborhood.

In 1978, a man-made disaster occurred. A gas-main explosion at the popular downtown eatery, the Kopper Kettle, destroyed two buildings, damaged others, and shattered the historic stained glass windows in the old Auburn Methodist Church. The Methodists saw to it that the stained glass was painstakingly restored.

Beginning about 1970, the city began to experience new commercial expansion that took place without municipal regulation. Like Topsy, Auburn "just growed," and often with unattractive results. For example, some developers began to bulldoze old neighborhoods and to pockmark the face of the city with stark, penitentiary-style barracks surrounded by solid asphalt parking lots. Indeed, not a tree or a shrub or a blade of grass survived in some developments.

By the end of the twentieth century, Auburn was far from being a village. The 2010 Census indicated that it was the ninth largest city in Alabama. When a village swells so very quickly into a city, however, it can experience growing pains. Sudden growth can alter a community's environment, disturb its surroundings, dim its ambience, dispense with its traditions, and take no notice of its historic character. In rapid urban development, far more is at stake than just the preservation of historic structures. In perusing this admittedly nostalgic record of what has been lost to Auburn, each friend of "the loveliest village" should look about our present city and attempt to balance the value of what is gone from our midst with the merit and importance of all that now has replaced it.

2

The College

As the city of Auburn's population has swelled, a local debate of some importance has emerged about whether Auburn is a university town or a town with a university in it. The authors of this book very decidedly take the view that Mollie Hollifield Jones described in her history of the town. Written in 1955, but still relevant today, "Miss Mollie" very eloquently declared:

> Auburn has been and it is hoped always will be a town of one major interest, a college center where men, women, and children speak the same language of devotion to its great institution and the welfare of its students. This attitude has caused a sense of solidarity; it is the very essence of our life, and its emanation, spoken of so widely as the "Auburn spirit," has carried to the far corners of the earth....

Because the changing names of the college do not come trippingly off the tongue, its friends and graduates since antebellum days always have called it simply "Auburn." However, from 1856 to 1872 its proper name actually was "The East Alabama Male College," a Methodist institution. When the state, with federal funds, took over the college in 1872, it became the Alabama Agricultural and Mechanical College. President William LeRoy Broun successfully proposed a name change to the Alabama Polytechnic Institute in 1899. Finally, in 1960, the legislature changed the name of the college to Auburn University, or Auburn, which is what everybody had called it all along.

Certainly the college has erected some of the town's most important buildings, and its faculty and its graduates have supervised the design and construction of many local landmarks. The university's early instruction in civil engineering and its pioneering establishment of a chair of architecture in 1907 have had an important local impact, as this volume illustrates in detail. This chapter offers some photographs and a few details to identify structures that once stood on the

Old Main campus of Auburn University but now have been swept away.

Old Main. On August 12, 1857, the village of Auburn celebrated laying the cornerstone of the main building of the East Alabama Male College, a newly-chartered, educational institution established and promoted by the local Methodist congregation and funded principally by subscription from the nearby area. Two exceedingly popular Alabama orators spoke on the occasion: the fiery Southern rights advocate, William Lowndes Yancey, whose oratory, it was said, struck like the lightning from heaven; and, the mellifluous Henry W. Hilliard, whose admirers vowed that they would travel the length of the state just to hear him pronounce the word, "Alabama." The Methodist Bishop of Georgia (George F. Pierce) presided over the day-long ceremony; he substituted for the Methodist Bishop of Alabama, who snubbed Auburn and preferred rival Greensboro as a college site for his denomination. By 1859, however, when the new building had risen and Auburn's new college opened its doors, the state's Methodist hierarchy had, reluctantly, reconciled itself to sponsoring two colleges in Alabama. Due to an error in a contemporary register of legislative acts, the college at Auburn and its historians for more than 150 years have celebrated an incorrect date, February 1, 1856, for the chartering of the institution by the state. Research for the present volume has revealed that the state actually awarded the charter on February 7, 1856.

Stephen Decatur Button, a nationally recognized architect, designed the tall Italianate-style academic building, after the college trustees rejected his far more elaborate (and expensive) design for a Gothic structure. Wary of cost, the trustees initially authorized only the expenditure of $25,000 for the building with its million bricks. In the end, it cost more than $60,000 (and its cost sometimes is reported erroneously to have been far larger than that). Despite the need for economy, however, a local trustee, Nathaniel Scott of Pebble Hill, convinced the board to require Button to include a chapel on the fourth floor.

Born in Connecticut, Button sojourned in the South in the 1840s and designed buildings that still survive in Montgomery, as well as in Columbus and Savannah, Georgia. He won a competition to design the Alabama state capitol in Montgomery, which was erected in 1847 but burned two years later. By the late 1850s, he had established himself in Philadelphia, where he practiced until his death in 1897. (He actually lived across the river in Camden, New Jersey, next door to the poet Walt Whitman.)

Button's Gothic proposal

Button's five-story buildings in Philadelphia used metal-frame (skeleton) construction that anticipated by thirty years the method later used in tall office buildings, and in the mid-twentieth century, architectural historians credited Button with influencing the advances in building construction of Louis Sullivan, the master of tall-building design (and the mentor to Frank Lloyd Wright). Besides his Philadelphia office buildings,

Button's best known surviving works are a significant number of highly-regarded resort structures on the New Jersey shore and an important Civil War landmark, the gatehouse to the Evergreen Cemetery at Gettysburg, Pennsylvania.

The towering gateposts of Button's Gettysburg entryway could be distant cousins of the two towers of his academic building at Auburn, and, like the gatehouse, the local structure had a role in the Civil War. When the conflict began in 1861, the East Alabama Male College suspended classes and had to abandon its main building. The roof soon began to leak, and trespassers presented a continuing problem. Nevertheless, in 1864, the legislature of Texas subsidized the building's conversion to the Texas Hospital, an infirmary to care for Texan and other Confederate soldiers wounded in the defense of Atlanta. The hospital was pitifully understaffed, and local women defied antebellum restrictions on the role of females by serving as nurses to the wounded men. In July 1864, when General Lovell Rousseau and 2,500 Federal cavalrymen raided Auburn to sever the railroad lifeline to Atlanta, local slaves gave the Federals details of the town's feeble defense. Led by sixteen-year-old John Hodges Drake (a drummer boy home on leave), a handful of recovering Confederate patients at the hospital offered token resistance, but most of the other patients who were not bedridden joined the citizenry in fleeing. Fortunately for the severely wounded, the Federal cavalry had no time to take prisoners and did not disturb the bedridden Confederates left behind.

After the war, when the nearly insolvent East Alabama Male College reopened in the fall of 1866, the trustees found the main building "very much injured by wind, rain, and mischievous persons." The financial state of the college grew even more precarious, and in 1872, on the motion of the first Sheldon Toomer (father to Auburn's beloved druggist, trustee, and bank president), the Alabama legislature accepted the property of the East Alabama Male College as the site of the new Alabama Agricultural and Mechanical College, federally funded by the Morrill Land Grant College Act.

Two student literary societies, the Websterian and the Wirt (both named for antebellum American political leaders) provided some continuity in the use of the main building. The societies furnished rooms that they filled with books and memorabilia, but all these materials, some quite valuable, were lost when the building burned in the early morning of June 24, 1887. The fire started in the chemistry rooms, perhaps set off by rats overturning inflammable liquids.

The college particularly regretted the destruction in the blaze of an oil portrait of Daniel Webster that the Mansfield Society of Boston had presented to the Websterian literary society in the antebellum era. The fire also destroyed a large mounted telescope given to the college by Professor John Darby, a distinguished antebellum scientist. One of Darby's successors on the faculty obviously regarded the telescope as a prize possession of the college. In one of the surviving photographs of Old Main, he is posed in a top hat, intently and somewhat stiffly gazing through the telescope on the front lawn. Although the loss of the building and much of its contents struck a heavy blow to the institution, volunteers succeeded in rescuing the main records of the college from the fire.

Students at the A & M called the main building Old Main, though in fact when the structure burned only thirty years had lapsed since the Masonic Order had supervised the laying of its cornerstone. By 1889, a new and more elaborate structure, now known as Samford Hall, had risen on the site. Although fire destroyed both Stephen Button's state capitol of 1847 and his Old Main of 1857, the foundations of the original buildings, according to tradition, served to support both new structures erected where the burnt ones had stood. Whatever the validity of such a claim, it is certain that today the cornerstone of Old Main can still be seen at the base of the northeast corner of Samford Hall. It serves as a reminder of a very proud moment in the opening chapter of the history of Auburn University.

Old Main Cornerstone

Broun Hall. Very appropriately, new Broun Hall has replaced the old structure bearing William LeRoy Broun's name. Indeed, at Auburn, Broun's name deserves always to be honored and recalled and pronounced correctly. It is "Broon," not "Brown." He had a vital role in providing armaments for the Confederacy and, after the Civil War, a long and distinguished academic career. As president of Auburn in the late nineteenth century, he balanced classical learning with courses that he introduced to the region, such as biology, electrical engineering and veterinary medicine. He adopted several newfangled notions, including the laboratory method of instruction and the elective system for students. With very little money to pay professors' salaries, he hired a remarkably distinguished faculty for the institution he headed.

Sympathetic to co-education, Broun directed Auburn to be the first college in Alabama to admit women into classes with men and, at a local literary society meeting, he once declared that women had achieved equal brilliance with men in the field of mathematics. In another epochal event of Broun's tenure as president, he permitted a history professor, Dr. George Petrie, to organize and coach the first football team in Alabama. Nevertheless, Broun denied the coach and the team any funds for their athletic activity. The college, he said, could not afford it!

A rather plain structure, the original wing of Broun Hall was completed in 1906. In 1910, however, a very elaborate central structure in classical style and a west wing were added to the original building. The architect for Broun Hall's enlargement was Nathaniel C. Curtis, who held the first chair of architecture in the Southern states, which Auburn established in 1907.

Curtis proved to be a very worthy occupant of the post. Besides establishing architecture as a solid academic subject, he designed a number of important local buildings that, unlike old Broun Hall, still survive, including Comer Hall, the Albert Thomas residence in Auburn's North College Historic District, and the original college library, endowed by Andrew Carnegie and now known as Mary

Broun Hall originally

Broun Hall with 1910 additions

Carnegie Library 1940

Martin Hall. Alas, a college architect has harshly altered the fine interior that Curtis designed for the old library.

In 1912, Curtis was appointed the first professor of architecture at Tulane University in New Orleans, but he kept a connection to Auburn through his marriage in 1914 to Nellie Thach, daughter of Auburn's President Charles C. Thach. Their son, Nathaniel Curtis Jr., also practiced architecture in New Orleans and has many distinguished buildings to his credit, perhaps most notably, the Superdome.

When the engineers left Broun Hall for more extensive quarters, various departments came to occupy the old building, which, in time, the college administration proposed to demolish. In the meantime, the administrators had provoked criticism by gutting Samford Hall's double staircases and destroying its Victorian interior. Perhaps as a result of the unpopular alteration of Samford, the projected demolition of Broun Hall encountered unexpected

Nichols Center

Top: Veterinary Building, 1898
Bottom: Veterinary Building as Alpha Lambda Tau, 1929

opposition. As a token gesture to the preservationists, the college therefore salvaged Nathaniel Curtis's classical Broun Hall portico and used it as the entryway to the Nichols Center, the new ROTC building.

Veterinary Building. In 1894, the college provided a building for its new veterinary department—a nine-room, two-story frame building on West Magnolia Avenue. Various outbuildings soon rose around the original structure, and to add to the bucolic setting of what is now downtown Auburn, Shel Toomer kept cows in his pasture across the street. By 1924, however, the vet school complex was relocated, and Ramsey Hall, the engineering building, was erected on the original vet building site. As to the old frame building itself, according to Christine B. Danner's 1950 survey of college buildings, it was moved and converted first to a fraternity house and then to a private residence.

The Early State Chemistry Buildings and Laboratories. In the nineteenth century, the impoverished college received important appropriations from the state legislature to employ a state chemist and to fund his work, much of which concerned analyses of the chemistry of the soil and other applications of chemistry to agriculture. Because of this special state funding, chemistry had more buildings associated with its early history than other departments. At an early period, the college had purchased the antebellum Levi Lee house, which stood at the present location of Biggin Hall. The chemistry department used the old house for many years, but its laboratory was located first in Old Main and was suspected of being the origin of the fire that destroyed that structure in 1887. Thereafter, the laboratory occupied its own separate building. Two small picturesque structures served in succession as the state's chemical laboratory. The first state chemical laboratory, a sturdy brick building raised on a high basement, had some decorative features that included stained glass windows and a small flat roof that may have contained a skylight. The laboratory stood next to the Lee house, and a greenhouse funded by the Extension Service for the study of plant diseases, was situated to the rear. The building served the state from about 1887 until 1900, when a second small building replaced it.

In the meantime, the college had been able to erect a substantial chemistry building, now serving a different purpose and known today as Hargis Hall. The second state chemical laboratory stood next door and had some architectural features, such as arched windows and some architectural details that closely resembled its larger neighbor. The state lab remained in the little building until 1929, when the department of applied art took up residency. Nevertheless, when Biggin Hall was erected in 1950, the college demolished the little brick structure that stood in Biggin's front yard.

Top: Levi Lee House as Chemistry Building
Bottom left: Chemistry Laboratory 1
Bottom right: State Laboratory 2, 1900

Faculty Row

All the houses on Faculty Row stood adjacent to the college campus, but they were privately owned. Now, however, the college has ownership of all these properties except the Drake house site; every single faculty residence has been demolished. Nevertheless, the names of the distinguished faculty members who once lived on Faculty Row should not be erased from memory. They earned an honored place in the history of the college.

Through the years, Auburn street names have changed confusingly. In the late nineteenth century, today's College Street was called Main Street, while College Street was the designation for today's Thach Avenue, which beginning in the nineteenth century was the site of Faculty Row. A map-index from 1893, prepared by the twenty-one-year-old Harry Hamilton Smith of the civil engineering department, provides a key to the faculty members who lived there at the time. Smith, who married a local girl, Maude Glenn, knew these residences very well.

The John Hodges Drake House (the Greenhouse). On the southeast corner of today's College Street and East Thach Avenue (then the corner of Main and College streets), stood a house that about 1900 had the distinction of being the first private home in the village to be wired for electricity. It was the residence of Dr. John Hodges Drake, the college physician and surgeon from 1873 to 1926.

Dr. Drake went to his office dutifully until a week before he died, and to the last he made house calls throughout the village by horse and buggy (or, more ac-

Drake House (Greenhouse)

Drake Infirmary

curately, by a little pony and buggy). In separating the wheat from the chaff and the really sick cadet from the faker, he possessed the wisdom of Solomon, and to both he dispensed pills, often mixed with bits of pipe tobacco, that he carried loose in his coat pocket. The faker received a strong laxative.

Despite Dr. Drake's eccentricities and his old-fashioned style of medical care, both Dr. George Petrie and Professor James P. C. Southall have left positive, appreciative accounts of the doctor's devoted medical services to them and their families. The doctor earned particular esteem for the unstinting care he gave to his patients in the deadly influenza epidemic of 1919, when so many lives were lost worldwide. At Auburn, seven hundred students contracted the flu, eighty of these developed pneumonia, and thirteen died. As the lone physician in this epidemic, Dr. Drake had only two trained nurses at his side. Nevertheless, as their mothers had cared for wounded Confederate soldiers in Auburn's five makeshift hospitals in the Civil War era, forty local women served night and day as volunteer nurses in this life-threatening emergency.

In tribute to his many years of devoted service, the trustees named the college infirmary in Dr. Drake's memory. As for the Drake house, it was converted to a boarding house after the doctor's death. Known as the Greenhouse, it served for many years to feed hungry students. Sad to say, however, the Drake Infirmary and the Greenhouse both have been demolished.

General James Henry Lane House. Opposite Dr. Drake's house, on the southwest corner of today's College and Thach, stood an antebellum home that was remodeled in the French Second Empire style and occupied after 1881 by

Lane House

General James Henry Lane, a professor of civil engineering who always insisted that he be addressed, not as "professor" but as "general." Raised to that rank at age twenty-nine, he had been, at the time, the youngest Confederate general; and, as he reminded the impertinent who addressed him incorrectly, he had served on the command staff of the North Carolina Brigade, which proudly claimed to be "First at Bethel! Farthest at Gettysburg! and Last at Appomattox!"

A native Virginian (and very proud of that fact), Lane had done well in a course in mathematics as a cadet at the Virginia Military Institute and had been chosen to serve as an assistant to his extremely eccentric instructor, Thomas J. Jackson, nicknamed "Stonewall" in the Civil War. The nadir of General Lane's Confederate career came when a sentry in his own brigade, by accident, fatally wounded Stonewall Jackson after his important victory at the battle of Chancellorsville. Lane nevertheless remained a friend to Jackson's widow and advised her on the biography that she eventually wrote of her husband.

The zenith of General Lane's career came when his men repelled the concentrated and deadly Federal attack at "the Bloody Angle" on May 13–14, 1864, during the battle at Spotsylvania Courthouse. Lane and his surviving men stumbled from the field still shaken from their twenty-four hour ordeal. They were making their way with aching footsteps back to camp when they recognized in the distance on rising ground a striking figure on horseback: General Robert E. Lee on Traveller. Realizing that their commanding officer had ridden out to meet them, the exhausted soldiers struggled to look sharp, get in step, and stop limping. However, they need not have worried. As they marched by their hero, General Lee doffed his hat in a sweeping gesture and bowed his head to the men of General Lane's brigade. It was a moment that the soldiers remembered and gloried in to the end of their days.

Happily for Auburn, the old soldier's house still survives, but the Auburn Woman's Club has restored it to its simpler antebellum appearance and moved it to a new site in Cary Woods.

David French Boyd House. In 1880, David French Boyd accepted the presidency of the college at Auburn and took up residence in a house that then stood far back from the road on Thach Avenue facing today's Samford Hall. Auburn's first Episcopal Church, noted for its listing steeple, had once occupied the site, but the building had collapsed after the Civil War.

The site proved unlucky for Boyd as well. He lasted only one year as college president, and when he returned to Louisiana, his wife, "Etta" (for Esther) stayed behind in Auburn with their younger children. Although their father deserves credit as the real founder of Louisiana State University, four of his children graduated from college at Auburn. Mary Boyd, Class of 1898, married Walter Linwood Fleming, perhaps the most distinguished of the many historians Dr. George Petrie trained at Alabama Polytechnic Institute (API). Her brother, Leroy Stafford Boyd, known as Lee, was working on his second degree, a master's in history, at the time of the map-index of 1893, which listed him in residence on Faculty Row. He also was serving as assistant in the library and secretary to the college president, William LeRoy Broun.

Through his father (a lifelong friend of William Tecumseh Sherman), Lee Boyd had influential connections in Washington and knew how to use them. With unusual agility, after graduation Lee took an active role in both Democratic and Republican politics. He subsequently served as assistant librarian at the Library of Congress and chief librarian for the Interstate Commerce Commission. He kept in touch with his alma mater through the years, but he did not persuade many of his fellow alumni that Auburn should abandon the injury-prone sport of football. Auburn University Archives holds an elaborate architectural drawing that he did, apparently as an undergraduate. It certainly is not the house he occupied on Faculty Row and appears to have been an exercise in drawing that

Boyd Drawing

he copied from an architectural plan book. As for the Boyd House on Faculty Row, its fate is uncertain. It may have been incorporated eventually into a complex of buildings used by the home economics department.

George Petrie House. In 1893, Dr. George Petrie won the hand of Mary, one of General Lane's very attractive daughters, and about the turn of the century, the couple built a house in the general's backyard on the north lawn of today's university library.

During his fifty-five years of notable service to Auburn, George Petrie made many enduring contributions to the institution. Despite low pay and an onerous teaching load, he undertook (without financial compensation and in his spare time) to establish and coach the first football team in Alabama, arrange its historic first game with the University of Georgia, create and play on the first tennis team, coach the baseball team, lay out Auburn's first golf course, organize a bicycle club, clear the way for two bicycle paths (one to Opelika, the other to Wright's Mill on Chewacla Creek), and create in the attic of Samford Hall, the first college gymnasium.

His contribution to academic excellence proved to be even more important. Among the earliest Alabamians to hold the PhD degree, he served as Auburn's first professor of history, where he introduced such innovations as the seminar

Petrie & Boyd houses

method, the use of oral history, and the insistence that students do original research in primary documents. A chronicler of the study of Southern history, Wendell Holmes Stephenson, has described Petrie as a "Pioneer Historian of the South" and lauded him for creating in a poor land-grant college in Alabama an "Auburn Oasis" of achievement in fostering historical study. Perhaps because of his personal magnetism, Petrie had a remarkable knack for attracting bright students to his seminars and classes, and they in turn under his direction produced research and writing that still has significant value.

Students with Prof. Petrie, including the future "Fessor" Parrish, beloved local principal, first row, second from right

On the massive porch of Petrie's wood-frame house, painted gray with blue trim, students and faculty and townspeople for many years gathered to socialize with the Petries. The photo of Petrie and an advanced history class, with some students hanging their legs over his porch, testifies to his special relationship with these young people, whom he always referred to as his "boys" and his "girls."

In 1943, in failing health, Dr. Petrie wrote the Auburn Creed, an enduring statement of belief for Auburn men and women. Distilled from his lifetime of service to the college, it remains his most valuable legacy to the institution he served with such distinction. Although buildings crumble and fall, Petrie's credo continues to be a legacy still treasured in Auburn today. It links his generation not only to the present day, but also to all generations of Auburn men and women to come.

Patrick Hues Mell Jr. House. On the southwest corner of today's Mell Street and Thach Avenue, stood the house of Professor and Mrs. Patrick Hues Mell, both of whom had an important place in the history of the college and the community. Professor Mell came from a distinguished academic family: his father was chancellor of the University of Georgia and the presiding officer of the Southern Baptist

Mell House and Bowling Alley

Convention. The younger Mell, who was a member of the Auburn faculty by 1880, served as professor of natural history and had wide-ranging academic interests. During his first years at Auburn, he taught geology, mineralogy, meteorology, botany, zoology, entomology, natural philosophy, telegraphy, civil engineering, mining engineering and French. Perhaps most importantly, he encouraged at Auburn the study of hybrids of American and foreign cotton, and for an exhibit he organized on that subject, he was awarded a silver medal at the Paris Exposition of 1900.

Mrs. Annie Rebecca Mell was the equal to her husband in local esteem. Besides playing the organ and leading the choir of the Presbyterian Church, she was a much-beloved hostess and friend to students, faculty, and townspeople alike. The young George Petrie left an especially affectionate recollection of her. Childless, the Mells opened their large house to students. Two of the entertainments they introduced to Auburn were Ping-Pong and bowling. In fact, they built a narrow bowling alley in their side yard.

Mrs. Mell founded local chapters of the Colonial Dames and Daughters of the American Revolution and held state-wide offices in those organizations as well as in the Alabama Federation of Women's Clubs, a pioneering organization that addressed public issues of concern to women. As vice-president of the AFWC, Mrs. Mell made a speech in Selma praising co-education at Auburn and advocating it for other colleges.

The College

In 1902, when Clemson University chose Professor Mell as its president and the popular couple left Auburn, the college purchased their house, an unusual example of high Victorian style. It was designed by Frank Judson Dudley, of the class of 1882, who trained as an architect at Auburn twenty-two years before a chair of architecture was established. His drawing of the house survives in the Auburn archives. After graduation, when Dudley inherited a flourishing lumber company in Columbus, Georgia, he apparently abandoned his architectural career.

The college first used the Mell house as YMCA headquarters. When the Carnegie Library (now Mary Martin Hall) was erected on the site, the Mell house was moved behind the new structure. Although very diminished in grandeur, the

Mell Plan

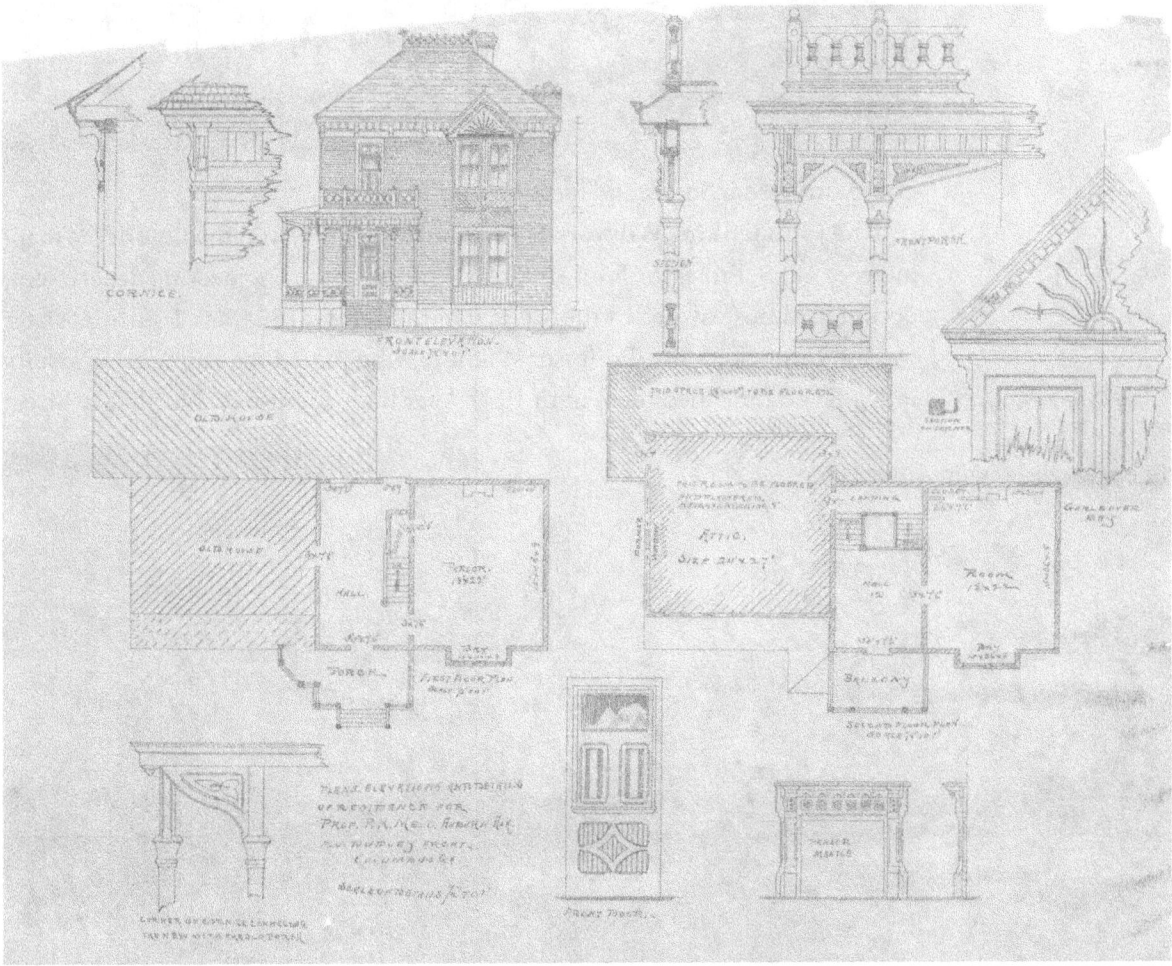

YMCA at Mell House

house survived in its second location for many years.

The John Jenkins Wilmore House and Mell Street. At the time of the map-index of 1893, Professor John Jenkins Wilmore, of the engineering department, occupied a house owned by the Mells. It burned about 1894, and Mell Street later was cut through its site. Professor Wilmore, who joined the engineering faculty in 1888 and remained there until 1937, later built a house on North Gay Street

Wilmore house

that still survives. An enthusiastic sportsman, Wilmore joined George Petrie in building not only a bicycle path to Wright's Mill, but also a roughhewn clubhouse where the bicycle club could hold dinners and parties.

The Charles Coleman Thach House. Originally, the house that stood on the southwest corner of today's Mell Street and Thach Avenue belonged to Alsea Holifield, grandfather of Auburn's historian, Mollie Hollifield Jones, who changed the spelling of the family name. Alsea Holifield died in 1893, and the map-index of that year identifies Professor Charles C. Thach in residence at the location. A well-liked professor of literature, whom students nicknamed "Cholly," Thach was elevated in 1902 to the presidency of the college. He was the first of Auburn's presidents to have attended the college as an undergraduate. When a president's home was built in 1914 (designed by the nationally important architectural educator, Joseph Hudnut and now known as Cater Hall), the Thach family was the first to occupy it. About 1919, their former home was converted into the college infirmary. About 1942, after the Drake infirmary was built, the house was demolished.

The Otis Smith House. When Mell Street was cut through from today's Thach Avenue, Faculty Row was extended around the corner. About 1901, Professor

Thach House

Otis Smith House

Mell built a house on the east side of the new street that he intended to rent out, but when he accepted the presidency of Clemson College, he sold the house to Professor and Mrs. Otis Smith.

Professor Smith was one of the most extraordinary individuals ever to be connected to the college at Auburn. Born and educated in Vermont, he came to the South before the Civil War, and fought long and heroically for the Confederacy. He served on the board of trustees of Auburn's East Alabama Male College and joined the faculty as a mathematics professor at the Alabama Agricultural and Mechanical College when it took over the former Methodist property in 1872. Uniquely, while teaching at Auburn, he served six years on the board of trustees of the University of Alabama. As a leader in statewide education, his most notable achievement was to convince the state legislature in 1872 to establish and fund a normal (teacher's) college for Alabama's former slaves.

A beloved teacher, he was celebrated for his absent-mindedness. For example, while holding forth on some profound question while smoking his pipe, he is supposed to have dumped its ashes in his pocket and thrown the pipe out the window.

Smith's wife, Antoinette, is here depicted reading on the porch of the house on Mell Street. Her daughter, Ellen (known as "Nellie"), married Charles Thach and lived just around the corner and then across the street in the president's home. The Thachs' eldest child, Elizabeth, married Nathaniel C. Curtis, who held the first chair of architecture at Auburn and in the South, but then moved on to New Orleans and Tulane University. Their son, Nathaniel Curtis Jr., a distinguished New Orleans architect in his own right, visited Auburn frequently and has left an unpublished reminiscence of the Smith and Thach families and old Faculty Row.

Daniel Thomas Gray House. Below the Smith house on Mell Street stood the Daniel Thomas Gray house. A Missourian, Gray served as head of the animal industry (now called animal husbandry) department in the School of Agriculture from 1908 to 1912. He then left Auburn for North Carolina State University.

Top: Gray House in 1911
Bottom: Gray House as remodeled, ca. 1922–23

The first photo shows the Gray house in its rural setting during Gray's first years on the faculty at Auburn. In 1921, he returned to the faculty as dean of agriculture and remodeled the house as shown in the second photo. He served as dean from 1921 to 1924.

Gray dealt successfully with two crises as dean: Comer Hall burned, and enemies of Auburn tried to move the Extension Service headquarters to Montgomery. To Gray's credit, he saw to Comer Hall's rebuilding, and he kept the Extension Service on campus at Auburn. When Gray left Auburn for the University of Arkansas, Luther Noble Duncan convinced the Alabama Extension Ser-

vice to acquire the Gray house to be used as a practice house to train extension workers in home economics. In time, the structure became the Commandant's House, the residence of the head of the ROTC. Spidle Hall now occupies the former site of the structure.

Dr. John Hodges Drake, General Lane, Dr. Petrie, Professor and Mrs. Mell, Dean Wilmore, President Thach, Professor Otis Smith, and Dean Gray lived on Faculty Row in a simpler time when the college was small and it was easier for students and faculty to intermingle. The affectionate reminiscences of these faculty members by their former students indicate that the closeness of the student-teacher relationship was enhanced because so many faculty members lived nearby—indeed, just across the street.

Alumni Gymnasium

In the late nineteenth century, the impecunious college at Auburn so urgently needed a gymnasium for indoor sports that a history professor, Dr. George Petrie, got together a crew of volunteers and improvised a roughhewn gym in the attic of Samford Hall. In the college year 1895–96, however, the college erected for $1,848 a one-room, frame gymnasium that stood three hundred yards behind Samford Hall.

Old gym

Because the state refused to appropriate public funds for a more adequate gymnasium, a lifelong friend of Auburn, Tom Bragg, took up the challenge. As president of the Auburn Alumni Association, Bragg had initiated the first homecoming event, and to solicit funds from alumni to build a new gymnasium he traveled up and down the state in his tiny auto.

The result of his labors, the Alumni Gymnasium, was dedicated in February 1916. Frank Lockwood, perhaps the state's best known architect at the time, designed the structure, and Thomas Purvis of Selma was the contractor. The dedication ceremony served as an important reunion for Auburn's athletic heroes, including "Tubby" Lockwood, a football hero and the architect's son (and in time an architect himself).

The gym stood across the ROTC drill field to the west of Samford Hall. A basketball court, which sometimes served as a dance floor, was situated on its upper floor, which had large windows. Balconies surrounded the court on three sides, and some of the most important entertainers of the first half of the twentieth century performed there, including Will Rogers. The gym also served as the venue for of a local showing of D. W. Griffith's 1915 silent film, *The Birth of a*

Alumni Gymnasium, with Bragg's auto parked in front

Nation, which almost provoked a race riot. Excited by Griffith's harsh depiction of blacks during Reconstruction, some college boys gathered at Toomer's Corner to exact local reprisals, but Auburn's winning football coach, Mike Donahue, in one of his finest moments at the college, calmed the students and put a stop to any potential trouble.

The building's basement held a swimming pool. Local lore holds that a young lady from Montgomery, Miss Zelda Sayre [Fitzgerald], once jumped into the swimming pool in her evening dress when attending a dance at the gym.

In time, the gym became completely outmoded for basketball games and swim meets. One of the peculiarities of the basketball court was a dead spot on the floor where a basketball would not bounce, but Auburn teams made a virtue of this defect by regularly attempting to maneuver their opponents into that position.

In 1953, the gym was hidden from view behind the new Student Union Building (now Foy Hall). With much larger venues available for indoor sports, dances and concerts, the college demolished the old gym when the student union was expanded in 1972. Nevertheless, for its architectural design by Frank Lockwood and for all it contributed to the college and the community in athletics and entertainment, it deserves an important place in local memory.

Graves Center

Graves Center honors Bibb Graves, "The Builder," one of Alabama's most progressive governors, who established close ties with President Franklin Roosevelt's New Deal and its many agencies. With the governor's backing, the college benefited from many New Deal programs that made possible an important expansion of the campus and its buildings. Not coincidentally, almost all the important buildings of the era were constructed to the architectural designs of Warren, Knight, and Davis, a Birmingham firm with very close ties to Auburn and to Governor Graves.

Indeed, in the important typescript record of campus buildings compiled by Christine B. Danner in 1950, she identifies thirty buildings on campus designed through the years by Warren, Knight, and Davis. Ranging from Ross Chemical Laboratory to the president's home, the firm put its lasting imprint on Auburn University. Furthermore, Warren, Knight, and Davis designed a very elaborate administration building for Auburn that was never built, but was to be named, very appropriately, for Governor Graves.

Nevertheless, Graves Center was not designed by Warren, Knight, and Davis, but rather by a distinguished member of Auburn's architectural faculty, E. Walter Burkhardt, who at the time also was directing the Historic American Buildings Survey in Alabama. The center was a less grandiose development intended to honor the governor. Eventually, it consisted of thirty cottages, an amphitheatre, and a central dining hall, before which a bust of Governor Graves was situated in an

Top: Graves Center Amphitheater
Bottom: Graves Center Dining Hall

encircling memorial. Because of potential vandalism, the bust of the governor has been removed to the college archives, and there remains at the original site only the empty memorial and the amphitheatre, made from granite setts, frequently called Belgian blocks, that once paved old Commerce Street in downtown Montgomery.

The Graves Center complex consisted of frame cottages, painted white, in a very simple, modified Greek Revival design, that fit very appropriately into their impressive setting, a stand of extraordinarily tall pine trees that surrounded the cottages and encircled the amphitheatre. The dining hall, also in modified Greek Revival style, served as a venue in the late 1930s for dances, costume parties, and commencement exercises.

Originally intended by the Extension Service to house conventions of agriculturalists, the Graves Center complex subsequently had many uses, eventually housing and feeding Auburn's football team.

Post-World War II Buildings

Today students, faculty, and townspeople can laugh at the makeshift, uncomfortable facilities that the college provided for returning veterans and their families after 1945. However, the veterans themselves, who had endured the hardships of severe financial depression and fierce global combat, welcomed the opportunity to obtain a free college education in a world at peace. They certainly exercised their right to complain about standing in long lines, but they shrugged and made the best of it, as their strong and indomitable generation was noted for doing.

When World War II drew to a close, Congress created the G. I. Bill of Rights to provide opportunities for a free college education to veterans of the conflict, many of whom became the first in their families to obtain a college degree. Since the prospect of sudden, significantly increased enrollments threatened to overwhelm the public colleges of Alabama, Governor Chauncey Sparks created the Commission on Higher Education to deal with the urgent situation. He named Auburn's executive secretary, Ralph Draughon, to be its director. Perhaps as a result, Auburn responded to the crisis more effectively and increased its enrollment by a larger percentage than any other Alabama college. Nevertheless, it took a lot of innovation and some very unusual solutions to resolve the complex predicament. To deal with its many headaches, Auburn fortunately had the unwearied and very popular P. M. "Mike" Norton, Auburn's coordinator of Veterans' Affairs, and Sam

Brewster, the can-do director of Buildings and Grounds.

The Deck Houses. Auburn's housing problems required innovation, and the most original solution the college came up with were the deck houses, actually the superstructures of tugboats, which the college acquired from the Federal Public Housing Administration in 1946 as U. S. Maritime surplus property. The notion of using the ninety-three sea-going structures for landlocked veterans' housing created quite a stir and received coverage in *Life* magazine, the most popular news periodical at the time.

Painted a light blue-gray, the deck houses had three rooms. Two downstairs rooms had two bunks each, and the upstairs room was intended as a study room.

The structures certainly were colorful but very tiny, and many veterans housed there felt like they were back on active duty in the armed forces. Somewhat embarrassed by all the attention the deck houses got, the college was glad to close them down and sell them in 1949.

Barracks for Men. Begun in May 1946 and completed by January 1947,

Above: Tugboat Town with bathhouse at center
Left: Tugboat deck houses

these temporary Army surplus facilities housed 570 single men. The barracks remained in use until 1952 when Bullard Hall, the annex to Magnolia Dormitory, opened. Modern, three-story, fireproof structures, both Magnolia and Bullard housed male students. (A new school of business now occupies the site where these dormitories stood.)

Faculty and Married Student Apartments. Sponsored by the Federal Public Housing Administration, the seventy-four pre-fabricated Graves Center student apartment units were contracted for in November 1945, two months after the close of the war, and were ready for occupancy by January 1946. In spite of their name, neither the Graves Center Student Apartments nor the Graves Center Faculty

Top: Postwar Temporary housing
Middle: Barracks, Student Housing
Bottom: Graves Center, temporary housing

Apartments were situated in Graves Center proper. The student apartments were located north of Samford Avenue, at a site that included today's Nuclear Science Center and Sewell Hall.

The Graves Center prefabricated faculty apartments were located to the east of the student apartments and also fronting on Samford. They occupied the site of today's Fine Arts Center. Moved from Panama City, Florida, on May 10, 1946, the fifty-one units were ready for occupancy by September of that year. Some of the faculty units, taken over by the fisheries department, survived until the 1970s when they were removed to make way for the Goodwin Music Building and the Goodwin Band Building.

The Student Activities Building. Erected in 1947, the Student Activities Building, once a combat hangar, provided another example of Auburn's use of war surplus materials to deal with the vast expansion in enrollment after World War II. Since the federal government gave Auburn a forty percent discount because of its many veterans, the college could buy the hangar for less than $10,000. It was large enough to accommodate the post-war student population and could seat three thousand people on portable metal chairs. Furthermore, it served many purposes, from dances to concerts. Lauritz Melchior, the great Wagnerian tenor, once thrilled his local audience by yelling a Danish "Var Eagle" as an encore. One respected leader of a chorale, Robert Shaw (later conductor of the Atlanta Symphony) actually liked to perform in the former hangar because it resembled a medieval cathedral in its acoustics. Sad to say, it also resembled a medieval building by being extremely difficult to heat in winter. Nevertheless, it provided a venue for many a festive occasion and even today provides former students of that era with warm memories.

The Sports Arena. Another war surplus facility at Auburn, the

Student Activities Building

Sports Arena   Sports Arena stood originally at Camp Livingston in Louisiana until it was dismantled and re-erected at Auburn in January 1948 at a total cost of $123,000. It had a seating capacity of 1,770, and for smaller activities with folding bleachers it accommodated 3,228. Basketball players remember it fondly because near the basket the wooden floorboards were spring-like and would give the shooter an extra boost when he jumped for a goal. More sophisticated venues did not provide the player with that extra leverage.

The Sports Arena had a spectacular end. At a home football game, a fan fired up a grill on the arena's porch and accidentally fired up the building as well. In full view of many of the spectators in the stadium, the Sports Arena blazed out of control, thus providing spectacular fireworks for a large number of excited fans.

Early Fraternity Houses: 1901–51

College fraternities have proven to be a mixed blessing for Auburn's architectural heritage. To their credit, fraternities purchased and thereby helped preserve some of the town's most important early residences, particularly those of the late Victorian era. Fraternities deserve recognition, as well, for building some of Auburn's most architecturally significant structures, such as the Phi Delta Theta house of 1912, designed by Nathaniel C. Curtis and William Warren; Curtis's Lambda Chi house of 1916; Charles Kelley's butterfly-roofed Lambda Chi house of 1951; and the many traditional but very elegant frat houses designed in the 1920s and 1930s by Warren, Knight, and Davis.

On the other hand, college boys have not made ideal tenants of these noteworthy buildings. Sad to say, Auburn frat houses do not have a long shelf life. Their tenants often have left them considerably battered and very much the worse for wear.

The earliest fraternities did not share living accommodations; they gathered in meeting rooms. In 1888, J. M. Thomas completed on the northeast corner of College and Magnolia a two-story brick building with the upper floor, called Thomas Hall, available "for public entertainments" such as the plays put on by Coach John Heisman's A.P.I. Dramatic Club in 1897–98. Fraternities also could rent space on the extensive upper floor for their chapter rooms, such as the ATO Hall, which the Alpha Tau Omegas furnished with elaborate fraternal insignia and emblems. When an alumnus of the ATOs, young Sheldon Toomer, assumed management of his stepfather's drugstore on the ground floor of this multi-use building, it was Toomer, rather than Thomas, whose name got attached to the corner where this much-modified structure still stands.

ATO Hall over Toomer's Drug Store

Besides their meeting rooms, early fraternities also had hangouts. On the southeast corner of College and Magnolia, a very popu-

Top: Students at Kandy Kitchen
Bottom: ATO Fraternity with Dr. Ross

lar and somewhat rowdy male hangout known as the Kandy Kitchen opened. It served only "soft" beverages since the town of Auburn maintained its nineteenth-century restrictions against alcoholic beverages well into the twentieth century. Nevertheless, the college yearbook of 1899 included advertisements for three whisky stores in nearby Opelika. Although the city of Auburn officially observed abstemious principles, fraternity boys (and a lot of the local population) regularly refreshed themselves by means of Opelika's whisky supply.

The college faculty in this early period established close ties with the fraternities and entertained them, on occasion, in their homes. Depicted here, for example, are the ATOs, on their very best behavior, posed on the steps of their host (and fraternity brother) Bennett Battle Ross, professor of chemistry, who is seated on the far left on the first row. The student body, not just the ATOs, usually voted Ross the most popular teacher on campus.

It should be noted, in passing, that the Ross House, where the ATOs posed, was built by Professor Ross's father, a Methodist clergyman, and it was many times altered and remodeled through the years. When the golden-tongued nineteenth-century political orator, William Jennings Bryan, was to visit Auburn overnight he was invited to be a guest at the Ross home. For this important occasion, Professor Ross installed an indoor bathroom, by tradition the first in Auburn. Alas, Bryan changed his plans at the last minute and did not stay the night, but the story of the indoor bathroom went down in local lore and was oft-repeated by Professor Ross, his family, and their many friends.

In 1901, the Kappa Alpha Order bought a lot across Gay Street from the Methodist Church. Soon thereafter the KA members built the first local structure specifically designed to be a fraternity chapter house. It resembled a family dwelling, and its best feature was a semi-oval entrance hall and a large wrap-around porch, where the fraternity boys liked to gather and to entertain. In time, the KAs vacated the building, and Dr. B. F. Thomas, a physician, purchased it, bricked it over, and turned the entrance hall into a waiting room for his patients. The building still stands in its altered state.

Fraternities frequently rented housing in the early twentieth century, but the Kappa Sigma local chapter became, after the Kappa Alphas, the second fraternity to own its chapter house. They did not build, but rather bought a handsome residence on the northeast corner of Gay and Magnolia, and by 1909 had converted it to their purposes. The house caught fire at 5 A.M. on January 9, 1915, but the fraternity remodeled it and continued in residence there for many years. In the late 1930s, when they moved to a new house on the southeast corner of North Gay and Glenn, a succession of other fraternities took over their original house on Gay and Magnolia until the AuburnBank purchased the property to build their new central bank at the site.

Kappa Alpha as built

The third fraternity to own its meeting place was the Phi Delta Theta chapter at Auburn, which acquired in 1912 a structure designed in 1910 and intended originally for the ATOs, who appar-

Top: Kappa Sigma
Bottom: Phi Delta Theta

ently were unable at the time to finance it. The architects of the chapter house were William T. Warren and Nathaniel C. Curtis, both of whom had been ATOs as undergraduates.

Warren, an Auburn graduate of 1897 in engineering, obtained a degree in architecture from Columbia University in 1902 and practiced thereafter until 1905 with McKim, Mead, and White, a preeminent American architectural firm. In 1917, he formed the firm of Warren and Knight, eventually Warren, Knight, and Davis, which designed numerous significant buildings in twentieth-century Auburn and Alabama. Including Warren's partner, John Eayres Davis (class of 1911), the architectural firm employed by 1929 a total of nine Auburn graduates.

Nevertheless, Warren's partner in the fraternity house project of 1910–12 was an Auburn faculty member, but not an Auburn alumnus. Nathaniel C. Curtis, graduated from the University of North Carolina, Chapel Hill, and went on to study architecture at Columbia University, class of 1904. When Auburn in 1907 established the first chair of architecture in the South, the college appointed Curtis to the post, which he occupied until 1912. He then went on to chair the new School of Architecture at Tulane and to establish an extensive architectural practice out of New Orleans.

A few snapshots of the Curtis-Warren effort illustrate the two-story central hall with a gallery surrounding it. The architects' preliminary drawings from 1910 do not include a kitchen or bathrooms and provide heating for the structure by a series of fireplaces. Nevertheless, the structure was frequently remodeled during its long life, and when the Phi Delts moved to College Street, the ATOs took over the house originally intended for them.

The fourth fraternity to own a house at Auburn (and the third to build their chapter house) were the Lambda Chis. In 1916, they built a house on West Magnolia Avenue that still stands but is now encased in a completely modern commercial structure; only its roofline remains visible from the street. Nathaniel C. Curtis designed the fraternity house. After his departure from Auburn, he continued to receive important local architectural commissions in the city, perhaps because in 1913 he married the daughter of the president of the college, Charles Coleman Thach.

Lambda Chi

World War I interrupted fraternity life in Auburn, but after its close, the college developed in 1922 a plan for the so-called New Fraternity Row, stretching along South College Street at the site today of the Auburn University Hotel and Conference Center. Bradford Knapp, as college president, received credit for the implementation of the plan, by which the college owned the building sites of the fraternities. By the new plan, the college also regulated the architecture of the buildings to create a harmonious ensemble of structures. Perhaps the college intended, as well, to regulate more closely some of the social activities of the fraternities, which were clustered in the center of the town and beginning to cause some local complaints. From their situation, north to south, the three fraternities that formed the original New Fraternity Row, were Phi Delta Theta, Delta Sigma Phi, and Pi Kappa Phi. The architects for these important structures have not been identified. The central structure, home of Delta Sigma Phi, faced the street, while the flanking fraternity houses, the Phi Delts and the Pi Kappa Phis, faced each other and had similar porticos.

The exterior detail of the Phi Delt house, the first completed on the row (in 1929) was particularly fine. Nevertheless, the house developed structural prob-

Fraternity Houses, Alabama Polytechnic Institute Auburn, Ala.

Fraternity Row lems about 1941 and began to settle. As it turned out, it had been built over a spring. (Perhaps it should be noted that in the nineteenth century a well in the vicinity of the future frat house provided an important source both for drinking water and for fighting fires.) Nevertheless, the Phi Delts remained in residence there well past the mid-century mark. When the house finally was demolished, an alumnus salvaged its strikingly unusual living room fireplace and installed it in his own home in Opelika.

The Delta Sigma Phi house soon followed the Phi Delt house to completion in the new row, but perhaps the severe economic depression of the 1930s intervened thereafter. The Pi Kappa Phi fraternity did not occupy its new house until the eve of World War II. The Alpha Gamma Rho house, a handsome structure, was also added later, facing the street, at the south end of the row. It did not detract, but in fact added to the harmonious whole that the college intended for the grouping of fraternities.

Soon after the college made plans for New Fraternity Row, it also approved plans for two fraternity houses to face each other at the bottom of the dirt road that became Mell Street. The handsome old Sigma Nu house, dating from 1927

Top: left, Phi Delta Theta; right, Delta Sigma Phi. Second row: left, Pi Kappa Phi; right, Alpha Gamma Rho. Third row: left, Sigma Nu; right, Theta Chi.

OPPOSITE. Top: left, Kappa Sigma; right, Sigma Phi Epsilon Middle: left, Sigma Chi; right, Kappa Alpha Bottom: left, Lambda Chi, 1951, with butterfly roof; right, Lambda Chi Alpha Interior

and now demolished, stood adjacent to what was known as Ag Hollow. It faced the Theta Chi house, designed by Warren, Knight, and Davis and completed in 1926.

The rear of the Theta Chi house looked over the old drill field, now occupied by women's dormitories. When the women's dormitories were built in the 1950s, a mistake in their installation made international news. To the horror of Katharine Cater, dean of women, the windows of the women's showers were put in backwards, so that the women could not see out, but the Theta Chis could see in. The mistake was corrected, but it provided a great moment in Theta Chi history and is still remembered happily by male students of the time.

Another fraternity row, not on college property, developed in the 1920s. After the Phi Delts departed for New Fraternity Row, the ATOs took over and remodeled the house originally intended for them on the northeast corner of Gay and Glenn. On the southeast corner of the intersection, on an extensive property where the Glenn family town house once stood, three fraternities, the Kappa Sigma, the Sigma Phi Epsilon, and the Pi Kappa Alpha built houses that stretched southward on Gay Street.

Although no longer a frat house, the especially distinctive Pi Kappa Alpha structure still stands and faces the intersection of Tichenor and Gay. The Pikes liked so much the design of this early house that they copied it when, years later, they built a new house on West Magnolia Avenue.

Two important local fraternity houses were not situated alongside other frats. The Sigma Chi house, completed in 1935, stood on the northwest corner of West Magnolia and Toomer, while the Kappa Alpha Order's house, occupied in 1942, was located on the southeast corner of Samford and College. Although time has somewhat modified their views, the KA Order always glorified its Southern connections, while the Sigma Chis even claimed to have a chapter in the Confederate Army. Perhaps these predilections explain the penchant of the two fraternities for large porticos in modified Greek Revival style.

Shortly before the Sigma Chis moved to their new home on West Magnolia Avenue, in 1951 the Lambda Chis built a house opposite them across Toomer Street. Designed by Charles Kelley, a talented faculty member of the school of architecture (and a Lambda Chi alumnus), the design featured a butterfly roof, which was higher at the front and rear eaves than in the center. It also featured an unusual fireplace, and, as an innovation for Auburn, a detached dormitory

for fraternity members. The present Lambda Chi house, of completely different design, now occupies the site.

Fraternity houses, of course, have become more like fraternity mansions at Auburn today. Once clustered, quite literally, in the middle of town, they have moved westward to new sites adjacent to Wire Road, where we can only hear them, from a distance, on weekends.

Perhaps we at Auburn have taken frat houses too much for granted. It is true that fraternity boys make a lot of noise, but, after all, their fraternity houses have served a very useful purpose. They have helped, importantly, in providing a solution to the perennial (and often very critical) problem of student housing at Auburn.

They also provided to the community in the first half of the twentieth century a rich and varied architectural heritage that has been almost totally eradicated. Fortunately, we do have photographs to record our loss and to remind us of all the distinctive fraternity houses that once lined our downtown streets. Of course, these photographs also quite pleasingly remind us, at least in retrospect, of all the fun and mischief that lively college boys have brought to our community through the years.

3

A Town of Schools

The Antebellum Years. Since its beginning, Auburn has been a town of schools. When Auburn's founder Judge John Harper led a party of Methodists to the area in late 1836, many of the settlers intended the new community to be a religious and educational center. Within a year, Auburn began to make this dream come true in a small way. On land sold by Harper, a land speculator, stood the log Methodist church, located on the corner of what is now East Magnolia and South Gay. The church doubled as a rude schoolhouse, where the town's first schoolmaster, Simeon Yancey, wielded the hickory stick of seminal Auburn antebellum education.

By 1837, the Baptists who had arrived in town joined with the Methodists to build a log schoolhouse on the lot that Judge Harper had sold them, across the street from the log church. The new school's notable teacher, Auburn's second schoolmaster, was "Judge" C. C. Flanagan. Evidence of the ecumenical quality of this educational enterprise is that both Baptists and Methodists sponsored the school and that its schoolmaster was Roman Catholic and had once studied for the priesthood. Flanagan taught at Auburn for twenty years and married the widowed Lizzie Taylor Harper, who had named the village.

The log schoolhouse probably had pupils of different ages and was a primary school emphasizing reading and writing and arithmetic. When the economic depression that began in 1837 ended at last in the 1840s, Auburn was able to open some secondary schools, but only a few of the early academies succeeded.

Most of Auburn's early schools were concentrated in a two-block area that extended from the corners of East Magnolia and South Gay north to North Gay and East Glenn on both sides of the dirt thoroughfare. For nearly a century, this area would be the site of a number of outposts of primary and secondary education in the wilderness of East Alabama.

By the 1850s, a succession of secondary schools for boys had opened and closed.

Finally, in 1857, Slaton's Academy opened on the corner of what is now Tichenor and North Gay. It served as a preparatory school for boys who expected to attend the East Alabama Male College. Its distinguished headmaster, William F. Slaton, was a prominent Methodist with influential friends, such as William Lowndes Yancey, A. A. Lipscomb, and James F. Dowdell. Slaton had been headmaster at the popular Oak Bowery Academy, Chambers County, but had been persuaded to come to Auburn when plans for the local male college were announced.

Likewise, no secondary school for girls prospered in early Auburn until Nathaniel Scott convinced the local Masonic lodge (Auburn Lodge #76 was chartered in 1847 and still exists) to support a female educational center. The Masons in the early 1850s had sponsored several secondary schools for girls in East Alabama including academies at Talladega, Tuskegee, and Dadeville. With Colonel Scott as president of its board of directors, the Auburn Masonic Female College opened in January 1853 in a capacious two-story, frame building where AuburnBank is now located.

The Alabama legislature chartered the school in 1853. Thus, its state charter predated by three years that of the East Alabama Male College, now Auburn University, making it the first college in Auburn.

Chapel of Auburn Masonic Female College. The college, after its first year, had 106 female pupils, some of whom boarded. The fees to attend seem modest by today's standards: $20 for the five-month session for a junior class member, $12 extra for each modern language, and wax-work lessons for a dollar each. Nevertheless the college was generally so prosperous that the Masons built a chapel adjacent to the school facing west on Gay Street, where the AuburnBank parking lot is today, at a cost of $2,500. A lodge meeting disbanded to attend the laying of the cornerstone of the frame chapel on October 1, 1853. It was said to be the largest auditorium in East Alabama, seating eight hundred people, according to the *Montgomery Advertiser*. Initially the college used the chapel for elaborate graduation exercises, which could include concerts "with six or eight pianos, flute and violin accompaniments." In 1860, the chapel was the site of a famous secession debate that is commemorated by a plaque now in the Auburn University Archives. The building also was the site of early co-education. When the Male College opened in 1859, many of its functions were held in the chapel. Also, some classes, such as chemistry, were held jointly at Old Main, the college building of the Male College. Advertisements in the two extant copies of the *Auburn Gazette* for the early 1850s, list such subjects as Latin and science being put into the heads of antebellum young ladies. In this case, the school probably was, in truth, a college. In the basement of the chapel, Professor John Darby, a chemistry teacher at the Male College, manufactured his famous purple-tinted Darby's Prophylactic Fluid, a useful antiseptic for treating injuries in the Civil War. Indeed, the chapel was a multi-purpose building, not just a site for spiritual comfort.

After the college was closed during the Civil War, the old chapel stood empty, and in 1883 it was moved to its present location next to Samford Hall (oral history says it was rolled the short distance on logs), where it sat in its Italianate guise until it was drastically remodeled in 1892 in the Greek Revival style and named for college trustee Charles Langdon. As Langdon Hall, the old building served many purposes—classroom, theater, as well as the location of the college-sponsored first picture show in town in 1912. The basement also was used for a variety of purposes. Home economics classes were taught in it for several years, but its longest use was as a student recreation center. The building is listed on the Historic American Buildings Survey and the National Register of Historic Places; it is the second oldest public building remaining in Auburn.

The only other reminder of the once thriving Masonic Female College is a plaque on a boulder to the left of AuburnBank. Placed by the United Daughters of the Confederacy, it commemorates the raising of the first Confederate flag in Auburn by student Betty Dowdell on March 4, 1861, simultaneously with the raising of the flag at the Capitol in Montgomery.

Auburn Masonic Female College Chapel

Auburn Female Institute

The Post-Bellum Years

In the 1840s, hardly a decade after the town's founding, there were approximately four hundred students in Auburn (some boarding in the town) and only about a thousand white citizens. Most Auburn schools closed during the Civil War, and in its aftermath, public and private schooling languished with the rest of the economy. The Slaton's Academy building became for several years a chair factory. However, at some point in the 1880s, the first notable post-war public school for whites moved into the rambling, one-story structure and became the Auburn Female Institute.

Auburn Female Institute. The town's first post-war public school, possibly begun as early as 1870, was located on Tichenor Avenue. It was a town school; that is, a municipal board of education governed it. Initially seven trustees were selected annually; in the early 1900s the terms were extended to two and later to five years. R. W. Burton, of bookstore fame, was an early school board member.

The school offered instruction in grades one through eleven under principal George W. Duncan. Subjects taught included English, Latin, history, science, literature, art, and drawing. The average cost per month was listed as Primary $1.41; Collegiate $1.91. Advertisements noted that excellent accommodations for board with families in the town were available at reasonable rates. In 1896, the school board appointed Miss Annie Heard to take charge of the primary departments, and the teacher of the second and third grades was Miss Leland Cooper, who later became the first female deacon of Auburn's First Baptist Church.

The Female Institute eventually accepted boys, and after completing the primary and intermediate courses, they could enter college as freshmen. Graduations, consequently, were all-girl ceremonies, and quite festive. In 1897, for instance, the six graduates wore white dresses for the occasion, and as each finished reciting her essay, gifts and flowers were brought to her on the stage. Gifts were such trinkets as button hooks, fan chains, or shoe horns; the flowers magnolias, water lilies, and garden flowers. The last graduation held in this old building was in May 1899. This same year a new school building was erected near the old one on North Gay Street.

Auburn Public School. The Auburn Female Institute was the one town school for white children almost until the end of the nineteenth century. Early in 1899, Mayor Charles Little and the town council issued bonds for $6,000 to build a new and larger schoolhouse. The contract went to J. A. Cullars of Auburn for $5,130.40 for a building 74x58½ feet that included a 40x70-foot auditorium on the second floor.

Even the best of new schools at that time were primitive by today's standards before water and sewerage systems were constructed in small towns. There was little "golden" in those school days of learning by lamplight, no plumbing or central heat. Designs for the new school were prepared by the Atlanta architectural firm Bruce and Morgan, already known in Auburn as architects for Samford Hall. Plans provided wood and coal pot-bellied stoves, but only an outdoor privy tactfully shielded by shrubbery. The cornerstone was laid on October 24, 1899, and the building was completed the following fall. Water was not provided until 1910 when the town council authorized necessary plumbing and "a bubbling fountain" for drinking water. As there was no cafeteria, students brought their own lunches, one of

Auburn Public School

the most popular foods being cold sweet potatoes. On the packed-dirt playground that had no equipment, one of the popular games was one-eyed cat.

In October 1907, principal Duncan, who also served as president of the town board of education, appeared before the town council to give a report on school expenses and attendance. The total of expenses for the year, with an average of 140 pupils, was $2,709, with $1,260 of the income from tuition fees, the town of Auburn providing $300 and the state providing $900. Duncan's salary was $1,080. This was for a town of approximately 1,450 citizens. Besides tuition, the schools in town got support from various sources, there not being a town school tax until decades later. There was a School Improvement Society, headed in 1909 by Dean J. J. Wilmore of the API School of Engineering.

By 1909, the school originally named Auburn Female Institute had become, more appropriately, the Auburn Public School offering eleven grades and a high school diploma. Auburnites considered it such an attribute to the small town that the large, rather gloomy school was featured on a postcard! For thirty-two years, this remained the consolidated school for whites in Auburn. After a separate high school was built in 1914, the old school remained standing as the seven-grade grammar school until 1931. After the high school was built, Miss Annie Heard was made principal of the grammar school. Always popular with her pupils for her scholastic enthusiasm, she once embraced a student for perfectly parsing a sentence, and exclaimed, "You have covered yourself in glory!"

Lee County High School. In 1914, an opportunity arose for Auburn to obtain a separate high school. Since 1907, the state had decreed that each county have a high school. In Lee County, the high school had been in Opelika. However, by 1914, the Lee County board of education decided to move the high school to Auburn and turn over the former Lee County High School building in Opelika for that city's own city high school, a practice that was growing with the steady increase in the number of students statewide. Auburn residents and town council heartily approved of the move from Opelika. The *Montgomery Advertiser* reported on May 5, 1914, that Auburn provided seven acres for the school, and the town council issued bonds for $10,000 to build a two-story brick edifice (the second floor served as an auditorium) with a tile roof, round-head windows on the second floor, and ample basement (but still no cafeteria).

Contractor Belas Hudson built the school for $10,400, and the new Lee County

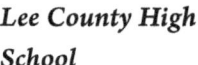
Lee County High School

High School opened for the 1914-15 school year with seventy students in grades 8-11 under its first principal, I. T. Quinn. In 1915, the legendary J. A. "Fessor" Parrish became principal. According to C. R. "Red" Meagher, Parrish began his duties with a meager budget of only $2,000 to pay himself and two teachers, and to maintain the large, impressive building. The first high school yearbook published (1944) was dedicated to Parrish, who was always highly popular with his students. He served as principal from 1915 until 1946, the longest tenure of any school administrator in the state at that time.

In 1931, when a schoolhouse accommodating all twelve primary and secondary grades was opened on Samford Avenue, the old high school closed, and was used as a recreation center. The next year, the old Female Institute building on Tichenor Avenue was torn down, and replaced by the post office (now city hall). By 1948, however, the old Lee County High School on Opelika Road was partially used again as a school, this time for sections of three grammar grades (two through four). One corner of the old auditorium was partitioned off as a fourth-grade classroom, while the rest of the second floor remained in use as the youth center. A popular weekend recreational place for teenagers, the youth center hostess for many years was the affable Mrs. O. P. South. The rest of the building served as the Northside Grammar School, until in the early 1950s when Auburn began to build other grammar schools. The entire building in the later 1950s and during the 1960s served as a recreation center. The first city swimming pool was built adjacent to it in 1953, but the building was finally torn down in 1973.

African American Schools

In 1961, all schools in Auburn became part of the city school system. By 1970, the entire Auburn school system was racially integrated. However, as in most towns in the American South, the post-bellum history of rigidly segregated schooling shows that the counterpart of attention to education for white children was inattention to the education of black ones. Decent schools for blacks were slow in coming; dates are few or nonexistent for the two oldest schools. The old town council records that go back to 1894 are the only, and often sketchy, official record for early black and white school information. School records for both whites and blacks only go back to 1942 for the county and 1961 for the city.

As early as 1866, the *Columbus Daily Enquirer* noted a school for blacks in Auburn established by a Mr. Whidby, an elderly minister of the Methodist Episcopal Conference, who ran the school at no charge to freedmen who wanted to attend. However, in the social and economic brutality of Reconstruction, schools for blacks were opposed by some elements of the white population, and the Columbus paper also noted that a black minister-educator named Alexander was taken from his home in Auburn one night and severely beaten. Scattered schools for blacks were established across the South by the Freedmen's Bureau, which was created by Congress in 1865 to deal with the education, medical necessities, and other problems of freedmen and indigent whites in the chaotic post-bellum period, when four million African Americans nationwide were suddenly freedmen.

According to one elderly black citizen, the first town-built, public black school was a one-room affair on Foster Street that offered only a few grammar school grades. The date of this school is uncertain. Before its establishment, most rudimentary education for blacks was probably confined to homes and churches; by 1903, there were two black churches in town: Ebenezer Baptist on Thach Avenue and AME Zion on Cox Street.

The initial one-room town school in Auburn was superseded by the Auburn Public School, on the corner of Bragg and Frazier, the only Rosenwald school for blacks built in the town limits (Auburn was not officially declared a city until June 1926, when, in a fit of pride, the town council summarily voted itself a city, boasting a population of well over 2,000). The Rosenwald Foundation helped to finance four schools in the Auburn vicinity—Lee County Training School just outside the town limits, as well as Mt. Moriah, Mt. Vernon, and Chewacla schools—and a total of fifteen in Lee County.

Such an arrangement produced the Auburn Public School for blacks. A meeting to raise the requisite local funds for a new school is reported in the *Montgomery Advertiser* on March 13, 1915, titled "Raise $1,000 at Auburn to Build Negro School." The "rally," as it was termed, was held at Ebenezer Baptist Church, and more than four hundred people attended, including about a hundred whites. Entertainment was provided by the Tuskegee Institute Glee Club. The campaign was led by the white Presbyterian minister, the Reverend J. T. Hutchinson. The newspaper article continues, "The colored citizens have contributed liberally and have raised in cash nearly $500 in the last thirty days. The town council voted $100 of the fund. With outside aid there is cash in sight to make the $1,000 complete."

The frame school was completed in 1917, originally offering seven grades, though it eventually included nine. It had five rooms, with the first grade being taught in the Prythian Hall on Frazier Street. A grand dedication was held on October 20th, according to an article in the *Savannah Tribune* for November 10, 1917. Julius Rosenwald was not present at the grand dedication ceremony, but Dr. Robert Moton, who succeeded Booker T. Washington as principal of Tuskegee, gave the keynote address that lauded Rosenwald. Also present were the Reverend Hutchinson, President Thach of the Alabama Polytechnic Institute, and a large number of other whites, according to widely published press accounts. Records held at Fisk University for Rosenwald schools show that $1,850 was spent on the building, grounds, and equipment; $1,550 of this was contributed by blacks, and $300 by Rosenwald.

A report on school expenditures in Auburn for 1921–22, for Auburn Grammar and the black Auburn Public School, was a mere $6,223.50. The county contributed $5,363, and Auburn only $450 for both schools. White principal Annie Heard was paid $900, and black principal H. L. Clark only $455.

This five-room school would serve as the town school for blacks until 1929, when it was superseded by a second Rosenwald school, Auburn's first black high school, Lee County Training School. Until the building of the latter school, blacks could not get a high school diploma in Auburn. They had to travel out of town to high schools in towns such as Tuskegee or Montgomery.

Lee County Training School

Lee County Training School. The second Rosenwald school for Auburn's black students was built just outside the city limits on what is now West Magnolia Avenue. At the time it was built, Lee County Training School had no formal address. Its location was known familiarly by blacks as "along the back line." It was, of course, in the Lee County school system, although the earlier school had been supported by the town, the county, and private subscriptions. It would remain the one school in the Auburn area for blacks until the building of Boykin Grammar School in 1951, followed by Drake High School in 1958.

A white man from Opelika, E. A. Screws, had donated the land for the school, part of the Pompey Foster estate in West Auburn. Foster was a well-known town barber and storekeeper, who may have been best known as the father of fourteen children. The method of raising funds for Auburn's first Rosenwald school was used again to erect the Lee County Training School.

The cornerstone of the school was laid in the fall of 1928; the Masonic lodges of Opelika, Loachapoka, and Auburn participated in the ceremonies. The guest speaker was Bishop H. S. Snow of the AME Zion Church, and E. A. Screws was given an ovation for his generosity.

The school opened with ten grades, was gradually increased to twelve, and the first principal was Clarence Jackson. The assistant principal was Andrew Jackson. According to Susie Hughes Giddens, a member of the first graduating class in 1932, "to distinguish them, we called them 'Big Jack' and 'Little Jack.'"

The red-brick building had four classrooms and a boiler room downstairs and four classrooms and a large auditorium upstairs. There was an outdoor privy, even though the county provided water to the school as early as 1929. In fact, indoor facilities never came to LCTS, as it was outside the city limits and beyond the extent of Auburn's very limited sewerage system that had been constructed in 1910. The elementary grades were taught downstairs; a portion of the boiler room was used as a cafeteria.

Lucy O. H. Miller, a student in the 1940s, recalled that when it rained, the "backline" school had the muddiest street in the county, and that not many families could afford a car, so most children walked to school, some as far as seven miles. School buses were not put on county roads until the late 1940s. In those years, the school held about 250 students, and family incomes were low, averaging $40 or less a week. Records at Fisk University show a considerably different financial picture for this latter school. Total cost for the school was $21,900, with blacks contributing $5,000; whites, $5,000; the general public $9,550; and Rosenwald $2,350.

Among the classes taught were literature, English, American history, biology, and algebra. At last, blacks in Auburn could get a high school diploma in their hometown. At the first graduation, held on May 19, 1932, there were six graduates, five girls and one boy.

The school closed during the height of the Depression, from 1932–33, but reopened the next year, with Lamar Player as principal. A later principal was R. E. Moore, who remained principal until Drake High School, a city school, was built in 1958. The old LCTS building remained standing until 1954, the venue for various civic and social events. Its site is now a park dedicated to Dr. Martin Luther King Jr., which is well within the city limits.

Adjacent to LCTS was the shop building, so-called, that housed classes in vocational agriculture and home economics. It was built with both county and state funds, and supplemented by money raised through various projects by Auburn and Lee County blacks in late 1939. Classes were held in it for the first time in September 1940. Unfortunately, however, the building burned, while

Lee Country Training School, Shop Building

classes were being held on the morning of January 14, 1941. According to the *Lee County Bulletin* for January 16, 1941, the principal, W. L. Player, estimated the loss at about $6,500. No one was injured, but tools, stoves, and all sorts of equipment used by the two departments were lost. The Auburn fire department went to the scene, but because the school was still outside the city limits and, consequently, about a mile from the nearest fire hydrant, there was virtually nothing that could be done to quench the fire. The building was a total loss and only partially covered by insurance.

Mt. Moriah School. Located on Wright's Mill Road near what is now the entrance to Chewacla State Park, the Mt. Moriah Rosenwald school was one of the one-room black schools in Lee County, but in the Auburn vicinity, when it was built sometime before 1932. More than Auburn Public School and Lee County Training School, it was typical of the rural Rosenwald schools built across the South. The one known photograph shows it in its decay the year before it was razed in 1962.

A story in the *Lee County Bulletin* for October 5, 1961, pictured and described the dilapidated state of the school that was still in use in the Lee County school system. The one room housed twenty-six students in grades one through six around a pot-bellied stove. The windows were broken, the roof leaked, the porch was rotten in places, and sanitation was virtually nonexistent. A corrugated iron outdoor privy existed for the girls only about a hundred feet from the rear of the school, but the boys were forced to use the woods. Drinking water had to be carried to the school from almost a mile away. A playground, as such, was nonexistent; any balls or play items had to be bought by the teachers. In an April 1961 report to the *Lee County Bulletin*, county superintendent V. C. Helms stated that of the twenty-nine black schools in the county, twenty-five were unfit for a good school program. They were housed any and everywhere—churches, lodge halls, etc.

According to the Lee County board of education, Mt. Moriah was to be abandoned after the end of the school year 1961–62, and "before that, if possible." Plans called for the students to be transferred to Boykin Street Elementary School in Auburn. Records at Fisk University show that the school cost $773; blacks paid $403, whites nothing, the public $100, and Rosenwald $270.

A longtime member of Mt. Moriah Church remembers the dilapidated school, and said that after it was torn down, the church was built on the site and took

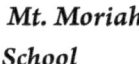
Mt. Moriah School

its name from the old school, a name that is a sad reminder both of educational neglect and of Rosenwald's much earlier generosity.

Epilogue

The entirety of a school, however, is not clapboards or bricks and mortar. It has little to do with plumbing or the lack of it. It has to do with the people who teach in them, and the students who study in them, whether sitting on rough-hewn benches or using laptop computers. What is learned in them is what lasts beyond the buildings that are lost. The old buildings pictured here are gone to time, but in the collective mind of their students, not forgotten. The dream of Auburn's founders, in spite of hiatuses during wars, civil and foreign, is sustained in Auburn.

Top: left, Presbyterian Church as built in 1851; right, remodeled as YWCA

Bottom: left, remodeled as Auburn Players Theater; right, remodeled as University Chapel

 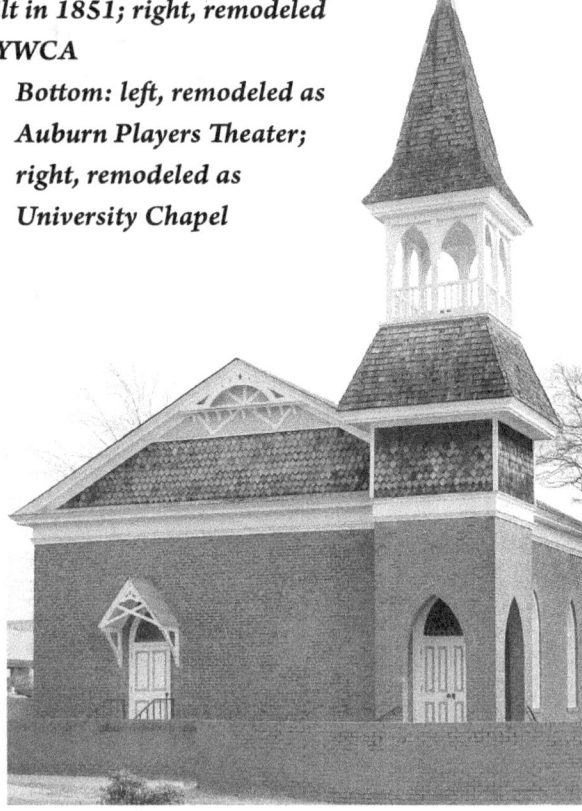

4

Churches

Auburn is fortunate that three of her historic church buildings have been preserved to welcome present-day visitors and worshippers—the Presbyterian Church of 1851, now the Auburn University Chapel; the Ebenezer Baptist Church of 1870, now the Auburn Unitarian-Universalist Fellowship; and the Methodist Church of 1899, now the Methodist Founders' Chapel. These remind us that many church buildings have served Auburn congregations for a time and then passed into Auburn history. Photographs preserve some of these "lost" churches; we know some only from descriptions in newspapers or church records or memoirs, some merely as locations on old maps.

In the images on the facing page, the evolution of one surviving building may be seen, from its original construction as the Presbyterian Church in the mid-nineteenth century, to its renovation at the turn of the twentieth century for use as the local YWCA "Y-Hut," to its adaptation for the Auburn Players Theatre in the 1950s, and finally to its present use as the Auburn University Chapel.

Methodists

It may have seemed at first that Auburn was a town for Methodists, but most mainstream Protestant denominations were represented among the citizens from Auburn's early years. Nonetheless, the Methodists were first out of the gate in church building. Their first, a log structure like most of the earliest Auburn buildings, was soon replaced in the 1850s by the modest neoclassical church, of which only one grainy image remains. This most stylistically sophisticated of antebellum Auburn's churches arose on what would become East Magnolia Avenue, where the present picturesque Victorian style **Methodist Church** of 1899 stands now as the Founders' Chapel. Remains of the earlier building, it is thought, are encased in the present one.

Although the image in the old photograph of the 1850s church is indistinct,

*Above: Methodist Church (1850)
Below: Hamill Sunday School Building*

its features suggest a Greek Revival style structure with a pedimented façade, a recessed entrance portico supported by two columns, and a nicely proportioned belfry rather than a steeple. Four tall side windows, presumably matched by four on the hidden side of the building, brought light to the sanctuary. Four corresponding windows on the side of a lower story confirm published accounts that the basement was usable, as Sunday school or meeting rooms or for slaves. No chimneys project above the church roof, although they are evident on the parsonage beside it. Early Methodism in Auburn may have offered fire and brimstone in place of heat in the building, or perhaps just cold comfort.

From its beginnings, Methodism has continued to thrive in Auburn. As the size of the first congregation grew, so did its physical plant. The Methodists put up one notable building in 1918, only to demolish and replace it forty years later in the 1950s. That was the **Hamill Memorial Sunday School Building**, named for Howard Hamill, an 1868 graduate of the East Alabama Male College, who was a

pioneer in modern Sunday school work. In the history of American Methodism, it has been suggested, "perhaps no other man of his generation had a wider influence in the field of religious education." The buff brick Hamill Building faced South Gay Street, next to the main church. Its architect, Professor Joseph Hudnut, who had designed the president's home on the API campus and who later became dean of Harvard University's Graduate School of Design, used a deliberately muted, stylized neoclassical vocabulary, a dramatic foil to the brick Victorian structure beside it. Still, the large windows did offer passers-by a handsome and eye-catching expanse of glass and the apsidal bulge in the rear wall of the building was unique in Auburn at the time.

Baptists

Baptists organized their first Auburn congregation in 1837, worshiping then, just as the Methodists had done, in a log structure located approximately where the present Auburn **Baptist Church** stands. No images of that early building survive, but a photograph of the building that replaced it probably in the 1850s, the second Auburn Baptist Church building, shows a neat and plain composition of steeple and rectangular assembly hall. Little distinguishes the building from scores of country churches across the South.

Baptist Church (2nd)

The Baptists soon outgrew this small sanctuary and with their next building decidedly distinguished themselves. Though still a frame building, the third Auburn Baptist Church building featured fine exterior woodwork—an open-work belfry, the triptych of arched windows at front and sides, stained glass—and soaring height.

The frame church served its members until 1929, when a conventional neoclassical church of red brick, the fourth Auburn Baptist Church building, replaced it, facing Glenn Avenue. The fourth Baptist Church building in Auburn is not entirely lost, for that structure is buried somewhere inside two subsequent renovations or additions.

Baptist Church (3rd)

Baptist Church (4th)

Presbyterians

Another mainline Protestant denomination in early Auburn, the Presbyterians, have worshiped in three church buildings, only one of which is "lost." The original church building, though hardly recognizable through several renovations and modernizations, still stands at the corner of West Thach and South College, and has become the Auburn University Chapel. The Presbyterians moved from that corner of Thach Avenue eastward to another corner of the same block, Thach and South Gay. In 1917, they constructed a neoclassical style building featuring identical recessed Ionic porticoes with properly proportioned entablatures on both Gay Street and Thach Avenue. The building was surmounted by a neoclassical balustrade on all four sides.

For Auburn, this church's sanctuary featured an innovative plan. The Akron Plan of the interior was not, to be sure, a Presbyterian idea at all; it was a Methodist innovation, first proposed for a Methodist Sunday school building in Akron, Ohio, in response to some new ideas in Christian education and worship services. The Akron configuration of church sanctuaries placed pulpit, choir, and organ either at the center of the long side of a rectangular space or in one corner of a square space. Auburn's **Presbyterian Church** used the latter. Rows of pews rose in curves from this corner focus, so each person in the same pew row sat at the same distance from the pulpit. Moveable partitions separated spaces at the

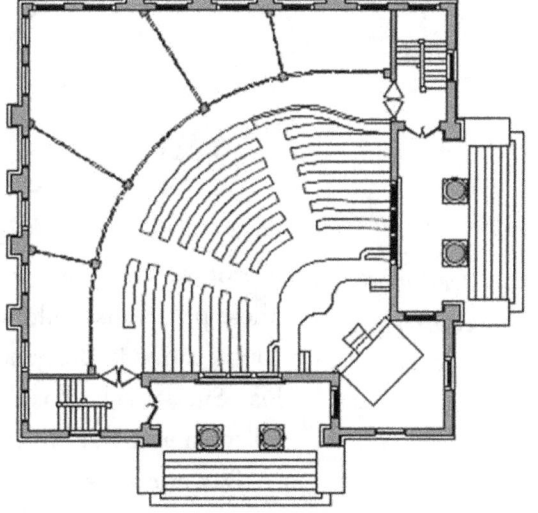

Presbyterian Church (1917)
Presbyterian Church Auditorium Plan

Presbyterian Church Elevation

rear of the sanctuary, which, when closed, served as Sunday school classrooms. These partitions could be opened when Sunday schoolers joined the rest of the congregation in the general worship service. (A nearby example of a true Akron Plan Sunday school is the semi-circular rear annex of the Opelika United Methodist Church, built in 1909.)

Blueprints used to construct the 1917 Auburn Presbyterian Church, uncovered in the present-day church closet, include the legend "MacIntosh & Leek, Architect." S. I. MacIntosh, contractor for the church, was an Opelika builder who was active in Auburn construction. He is credited, among other projects, with a house built on Glenn Avenue for the legendary "Fessor" Parrish, longtime principal of Lee County High School. Nothing, however, has been learned about Mr. Leek. His name does not appear in any local source so far discovered. Speculatively, he may have been the designer of a published plan adapted by MacIntosh and the Presbyterians, rather than the creator of a plan especially for this church at this time.

Episcopalians

Though Episcopalianism came to Auburn in 1851, it had but a tenuous foothold in the community, to judge by the early record of its church building. The first Episcopal Church stood on West Thach Avenue, just east of the present site of Auburn University's Mary Martin Hall, originally a Carnegie library. No photograph of the church is known, but its fate was prominently reported in the area press in 1876, its demise an occasion for both sour commentary and poignant remembrance. In the same year, the *Opelika Observer* of April 20 carried a notice of the auction of lumber and bricks from the abandoned Auburn Episcopal Church.

A hiatus in the record of the Episcopal congregation omits the events that doomed the rest of the building after the steeple blew down, but in 1887 the parish built another sanctuary on the south side of East Magnolia Avenue. The **Church of the Holy Innocents**, as it was consecrated, appeared in the Carpenter Gothic style, very fashionable in ecclesiastical architectural circles at the time. The board-and-batten exterior marked it as a country church, fitting charmingly into small-town Auburn of the late nineteenth century. Attached to the sanctuary space of the building was a rear wing, projecting to the east. In 1925, the old church was replaced by a brick structure (now St. Dunstan's Episcopal College Center).

Episcopal Church of the Holy Innocents

Roman Catholics

According to Auburn legend, Roman Catholicism came to Auburn to meet the spiritual needs of numbers of cadets at the Alabama Male Institute who

professed the Roman Catholic faith—a student subterfuge to avoid mandatory church attendance as there was no Roman Catholic congregation in the town. To fill the spiritual vacuum, the Opelika Catholic parish rose to the occasion and organized an Auburn outreach. The Auburn Catholic community grew from this unpromising beginning. In 1912 it built its first sanctuary, the **Church of the Sacred Heart** on East Magnolia Avenue, on the site of the present building that has until recently been known as **St. Michael's Roman Catholic Church**. Two buildings so different could hardly be imagined. Unlike the modern St. Michael's, designed by Auburn's Professor Walter Burkhardt, Sacred Heart was firmly in the neoclassical style that vied with Gothic as the appropriate ecclesiastical architectural style through the nineteenth and early twentieth centuries. No record has yet been found to identify the architect or the builder of Church of the Sacred Heart.

Top: Catholic Church of the Sacred Heart Bottom: St. Michael's Catholic Church

Dark brick gave the church a sober appearance. However, the projecting portico supported by four Ionic columns under a balustrade and dentil molding in the cornice surrounding the entire structure contributed to a quite stylish presence for this small building. It had unusual windows consisting of two parts separated by a wide middle panel, all hung in the same opening with sill below and header above to frame the three-part composition. A stone string course ran at main floor level above basement story windows. The main entrance to the sanctuary sat well above grade, approached by three steps from the sidewalk and another ten as one approached the entrance.

(Local scuttlebutt has it that the Presbyterians asked Walter Burkhardt to design the new church they planned to build in 1952. They rejected the modern design that he first proposed, but accepted his substitute design, the conventional neoclassical church that they built on the corner of Thach and Gay. In 1988, Auburn's Catholics enlisted Burkhardt to design a new church for them. Burkhardt, it is said, revived his earlier modern design; the Catholic parish built it as St. Michael's and took great pride in worshiping in one of Auburn's signature Burkhardt buildings.)

St. Martin de Porres Mission Chapel

In late 2009, the Auburn Catholic community moved into yet another new church, located north of the city, and sold their Burkhardt treasure to the neighboring Methodist congregation that has adapted it for Protestant purposes.

The Auburn Catholic community organized the **St. Martin de Porres Mission** in northwest Auburn in 1953. The mission chapel, shown above with communicants gathered in front, was located between Donahue Drive and Boykin Street. After the mission closed in 1974, the building was used for clothing distribution and as a day-care center.

African American Churches

While there is some anecdotal support for the belief that enslaved African Americans were given religious instruction and attended regular church services in specially reserved sections of Auburn churches, little documentary evidence

exists to construct a reliable history of the subject. What is certain and can be documented is that on Emancipation, African Americans launched themselves into church organizing and church building that has been vigorous to the present day. As already suggested, the surviving **Ebenezer Baptist Church** building is a standing reminder of that vigor. Church members built the structure in the late 1860s on land donated by a white friend. They built it of logs, covered with weatherboarding. The Baptist congregation worshiped in this building until 1969. It is now home to the Auburn Unitarian-Universalist Fellowship.

Auburn fortunately has not lost the Ebenezer Baptist Church, but two other African American church buildings have been lost, although their congregations thrive today in other structures. The older of the two was the AME Zion Church, organized in 1903. According to the 1928 Sanborn Fire Insurance map of Auburn, it was located on Cox Street. Surprisingly no photograph of any building at this location has been found, even though church histories suggest that it occupied this location into the 1940s.

Top: Ebenezer Baptist Church
Bottom: St. Luke CME Church

More fortunately, the demolished building of the **St. Luke CME Church** does survive in photographs. The building stood at the western edge of Auburn on a corner of West Glenn Avenue. Most westbound vehicles turned at this corner, passing the church and the minister's white weatherboard cottage facing Donahue Drive (once Acton Court), before crossing the railroad tracks and proceeding west to Loachapoka. Though not highly ornamented, the front of the building was carefully composed with major and minor tower blocks flanking a covered portico that was the main entrance. This format of two unequal corner towers occurs frequently in African American churches, both urban and rural. Stained glass filled the front and side windows. The building was replaced on the same site in 1981 with the present brick structure. The cornerstone of the original building is incorporated in a bell tower that rises in front of the newer church.

Late Twentieth Century Losses

Auburn Church of Christ. A major loss from Auburn's church building scene was the Church of Christ located on East Glenn Avenue. Auburn Professor Sidney Wall Little, who later became dean of the College of Architecture at the University of Arizona, designed the building. After first holding its services in the Tiger Theater auditorium, the congregation moved into the classroom structure that became the rear section of the church while the main portion of the building was still under construction. As the architect's presentation drawing and contemporary photographs show, the building was not pretentious, though it was imposing enough due to its size and elevated position above the street. Some departures from the conception in the drawing are noticeable. At some point, the belfry was removed, and the pitched roof extended over the wings. The church has no easily defined style; for 1940, when it was built, "contemporary" would have done.

Church of Christ

When the congregation moved to its present location on South College Street, they sold the original building to an Auburn Methodist congregation. Photographs from that period show that a belfry, which does not apparently conform to Little's original design, was added to the roof. The Methodist congregation eventually moved to a new facility farther from the center of town. The building fell into disrepair. The Checkers drive-in restaurant chain acquired the property and demolished the church to provide more

parking, better drive-in service access, and greater outdoor dining opportunities for its well-fed patrons.

Lakeview Baptist Church. Lakeview Baptist Church took its name from an original location on the edge of the Lakeview Subdivision, one of Auburn's earliest. Originally a mission of the First Baptist Church, the congregation grew rapidly, occupying a church building in contemporary design constructed in 1970 by the Auburn contractors, Shannon, Strobel and Weaver.

The building stood on the site now occupied by the Auburn city library, the

Lakeview Baptist Church
Village Christian Church

corner of East Thach and Dean. By the mid 1990s, a burgeoning membership required moving to an expanded facility at the corner of University and East Glenn. From neither the older nor the newer building, it seems, was a lake in view.

Village Christian Church. A Disciples of Christ congregation was organized in Auburn in the first decade of the twentieth century. According to church records, at one time Milligan Earnest, a prominent citizen and manager of the A&P grocery store, preached monthly to this congregation. Not until 1956-57 did the members meet in their own church building. The Village Christian Church, as it was known, was located on Cox Street, with a parsonage nearby. In 1989 the church building was sold to a developer who built student apartments on the site, while the Village Christian Church relocated to a new site on University Drive.

Church-Related Buildings

The early photograph of the Methodist Church (see page 62), shows a home for the parson nearby, built after the Civil War. For a time, this was a typical practice for most Auburn churches. That Methodist parsonage shown was a typical house for the period in this place. So it was likewise for other churches in providing accommodations for their ministers. The Methodists built at least one other parsonage next to their church, according to newspaper reports, though we have not identified any photograph of it. Later on, a Methodist parsonage was located on the west side of South Gay Street. In fact, two Methodist parsonages were located in that block, one for the local minister and another, the District Parsonage, for the presiding elder of the Montgomery District. This building was sold in 1902 when the seat of the presiding elder was relocated to Montgomery. All of the houses on the west side of this block of South Gay Street have been removed. The Methodist parsonages—and a great deal more—thus are "lost."

The Baptists, too, located their minister's residence near the sanctuary, although whether this was their practice from the beginning is not known. The counterpart to the Methodist parsonage was the Baptist pastorium, just to the east of the First Baptist Church facing Glenn Avenue. It appears to have been a Colonial Revival style, two-story house, sited near the street. The building was removed to accommodate expansion of the church campus.

The modesty of the Episcopal Church of 1887 is not matched by the Episcopal rectory, for it seems to have been a large house when compared with the size of

Presbyterian Manse

the church. The rectory was built in 1900 and remained in place after a new church arose beside it.

For Presbyterians, the minister's house is the Presbyterian manse. In a more-or-less Dutch Colonial style, it was built to the west of the 1917 church. Though the building is lost from the Auburn cityscape, it was fortunately moved to a county site rather than demolished.

The same good fortune did not come to another Presbyterian-related building, the house just north of the church facing South Gay Street that became known as Westminster House, used principally for college outreach activities. The property, purchased from the Blasingame family and once known as Hornsby Hall, was at one time the home of William LeRoy Broun, who became president of the Alabama Polytechnic Institute (see also pages 93–94). The Presbyterians

Left: Westminster House (formerly Hornsby Hall)
Below: St. Luke CME Parsonage
Bottom: Village Christian Church Parsonage

ultimately demolished the building to expand the church campus.

We know of only one other minister's house located next to a church. That was the cottage next to the St. Luke CME Church. It was removed at the time the old church was demolished to make way for the new building.

The parsonage for the Village Christian Church (Disciples of Christ) was located near, but not adjacent to, the church sanctuary on Cox Street.

Thomas and Lizzie Taylor Harper House

5

Early Period Houses

The settlers of Auburn in 1836 built their first rude homes, according to Auburn historian Mary Reese, "in fields where generations of Creek Indians slept." By the late 1840s, more substantial houses, sometimes built in Greek Revival style, had replaced these first wilderness homes. What explained such a transition from Indian huts and log cabins to two-storied, sometimes columned dwellings?

The new era of house building was based on cotton, so productive in the Deep South climate that it could support at least a few grand houses and numerous slaves, as well as the more common modest establishments of yeoman farmers and townsmen spreading over cotton country.

The unexpected sophistication of the Greek Revival style in an otherwise rude wilderness was a local expression of a national enthusiasm for the Hellenic. Wealthy Deep South plantation owners in particular, considered themselves, however naively, the heirs of the grandeurs of Grecian architecture and culture, while a vernacular expression of the style was to be found in domestic, commercial, and institutional buildings all over the country, not just in the South.

By the mid-1840s, the style was firmly established as emblematic of the antebellum South. Broad porches, sometimes surrounding the whole house, and wide central halls, twelve- to fourteen-foot ceilings, and numerous tall windows also had a more practical purpose: to temper the Southern heat. Large houses also accommodated the large families typical of that era, households that usually were maintained by slaves. The columned style with a distinctive hipped roof was early seen in businesses as well as homes, and numerous adaptations occurred over the decades before and after the Civil War. The owners ranged from wealthy planters to modest innkeepers, and the houses were found as the centers of plantations and as fine town houses in the middle of the small business districts, whose owners had plantations beyond the limits of the towns.

Auburn's antebellum buildings have fallen to a variety of destructive forces—fire, tornado, neglect, greed. Houses, perhaps, are among those losses most deeply felt. Largely through the efforts of Walter Burkhardt, the pioneer figure in Alabama's participation in the Depression-era Historic American Buildings Survey (HABS), and through newspaper articles about his project written by Mrs. Burkhardt, under the name of Varian Feare, at least a partial record of the early homes in Auburn has been handed down to Auburn's architecture and history buffs of today.

Thomas and Lizzie Taylor Harper House. The earliest house known to have been preserved in a photograph (see page 76) was the home of Thomas and Lizzie Taylor Harper on what is today the west side of North College Street. The exact year of its construction and the name of the builder are uncertain, although the late 1830s is a likely date. Reportedly, it was the first frame house to rise in the village that had been dominated by log construction. The building appears from the photograph to have been an "I-house," three bays wide, one room deep, two stories high, a standard house form through the United States, not just in the South. The house was demolished about 1900.

Christopher and Lizzie Harper Flanagan House. By tradition, the Flanagan House dated from Auburn's earliest years and encased a log cabin hidden in a wooden, one-story Greek Revival style house that was built around it. There

C. C. Flanagan House

does not seem to be any documentation to support the log cabin tradition, but the Greek Revival structure is clearly evident in the surviving photographs, even though a later owner added an ungainly second story to the house.

Nevertheless, plentiful documentation attests to the historic associations of the house. Two of the earliest and most important figures in Auburn's history lived there. Christopher Flanagan was born in Ireland and trained for the priesthood, but came to Auburn as the village's second schoolmaster. Thomas Harper, son of Auburn's founder, actually recruited Flanagan, and after Harper's early death in 1843, Flanagan married his sponsor's widow, Lizzie Taylor Harper, who had named Auburn. The extraordinarily lengthy full name of the bride then became Elizabeth Jordan Whitehead Taylor Harper Flanagan.

After the Flanagans wed, they lived in this house, which stood on East Magnolia Avenue between the original bounds of the Methodist Church and just above the site of the Roman Catholic Church of 1912. It is presumed that Flanagan remained Catholic and that Lizzie converted, and it seems a remarkable coincidence that the two most prominent Catholics in an overwhelmingly Protestant community should live next door to the site of the first Catholic church.

Lizzie had two children by her first marriage and two by her second. Furthermore, about 1845 the Flanagans invited their orphaned niece, Alicia Milton of New Orleans, to join their household. She arrived with her nurse, Gatsy Rice, a slave. Both Alicia and Gatsy were to become Auburn institutions: Alicia was a popular teacher, and Gatsy was a laundress and seamstress to college cadets.

The Flanagan House attracted very little interest from preservationists, and, so far as is known, no architectural historian ever examined the structure. Nevertheless, in spite of its awkward exterior, the colorful figures associated with the house make it worthy of local note.

Edwin Reese House. Edwin Reese claimed to be the only Presbyterian in early Auburn, but somewhat paradoxically the sturdy brick church that he built for his meager congregation in 1850 is the town's only surviving antebellum church building, Auburn's first known building of brick construction, and the oldest public building still standing in today's city. It serves now as Auburn University Chapel.

The church building is Reese's only monument. Rather than tombstones in Pine Hill Cemetery, his family marked their cemetery lot with a special wrought iron fence and placed a memorial stained glass window in the family's church.

Mary Tippins at the Reese-Wright House

Vandals have stolen the fence, and the location of the church window is unknown; it may have been moved to one of the Presbyterian churches that the Reese family endowed in the Chattahoochee valley. Furthermore, the substantial antebellum home that Edwin Reese built at today's 524 Wright's Mill Road has disappeared almost without a trace, having burned in 1929.

Reese's various enterprises testify to his versatility and talent as a businessman. He had an economic interest in local mercantile establishments; he had a large plantation outside Auburn; but, according to his daughter, his chief source of income came from selling lime from the vicinity of today's Chewacla State Park. Indeed, Reese even discovered a seam of marble in his investigation of the Chewacla Creek area.

Sad to say, the substantial income he earned from selling lime was dissipated, according to his daughter, by his morphine addiction, which he acquired in ill health at an early age and never was able to give up. Particularly during the Civil War, when morphine was very scarce, he had to pay enormous sums to supply his addiction.

The Reese House was built about 1850, and from the only photograph we have it bears some resemblance to other Auburn structures of the period, such as the McElhaney-Jones Hotel and the White-Harris House. Reese's large immediate and extended family occupied the house, and during the Civil War the family took in wounded soldiers who had recuperated enough so that they were not confined to local hospitals.

The Reese family's fortunes declined after Appomattox, and at the beginning of the twentieth century, Thomas Oscar Wright bought the house. Nevertheless, by 1929 both Wright and his widow had died, and another large family, the lively and popular Tippinses, rented the house. Luckily, one of their photographs provides us with the only known peek at the Edwin Reese antebellum structure.

After fire destroyed the house, T. O. Wright's son, Leslie, seems to have assumed development of the surrounding acreage. To the south of the Reese House site, he built his own substantial house, and, farther along, he laid out Virginia Avenue and named it after a favorite niece, Virginia Williamson Prestridge.

Evidence of the Edwin Reese House, notable locally for its architecture and its historic associations, was until the publication of this book, almost completely lost. But now, with the help of the Tippins family, *Lost Auburn* can provide readers today with at least a glimpse of the old house and a few details of its long and important history.

Perry-Cauthen House. The violent and unintended destruction of the Perry-Cauthen House on East Drake Avenue was both an architectural and historical loss. The building suffered irremediable damage in a devastating tornado in April 1953 that wreaked destruction on much of north Auburn.

Built between 1855 and 1860, the house was a Greek Revival style structure of two stories, with a low hipped roof and front portico, and with kitchen and

Perry-Cauthen House

dining room on the lower floor. The raised-cottage house form was uncommon in the Auburn area. Only two raised cottages are known to have been built in the town. (The other, the Cary-Pick House on North College Street, still stands.)

The builder, Simeon Perry, played a major part in the formation of early Auburn. A civil engineer and a member of the settlement party in 1836, he laid out the metes and bounds of the earliest Auburn, one mile square. Perry prospered in the new village he had limned. He became a large land and slave owner. For several years, he served as intendent (mayor). The short, side street in front of the site of the Perry-Cauthen House still bears his name. When Mrs. Cauthen, a longtime resident of the house, formed a garden club, she named it for Perry. The Perry Garden Club still exists today.

Drake-Samford House. Historically, the Drake-Samford House was the site of the marriage of Caroline Drake to William James Samford, who became governor of Alabama and for whom Auburn University's Samford Hall is named. After 1857, this was the home of Confederate veteran John Hodges Drake Sr., whose son, John Hodges Jr., was the college's first physician, serving fifty years. The son accompanied his father to war as a sixteen-year old drummer boy.

Perhaps the worst loss of an antebellum house in the later twentieth century was the destruction of the Drake-Samford House on the corner of North Gay

Drake-Samford House; stair

and East Drake, only a block from the Perry-Cauthen House. Its loss was of a far different nature. This 1850s house was razed in 1978 by contractor Jack Bailey who intended to build apartments on the lot that was dotted with cedar trees. His dreams fell through; all that remains today on the empty lot is a lone cedar.

The house was an antebellum architectural treasure, the home of famous owners in the community and state. Two-story, clapboard with typical hipped roof and large four-columned front portico, it also featured a beautiful, winding mahogany staircase that was destroyed with the rest of the building.

The photographs of the Drake-Samford House are two of the many that Auburn professional photographer W. N. Manning produced for Professor Burkhardt's HABS project.

McElhaney House (Jones Hotel). A second of the four Auburn houses documented by the HABS was the McElhaney-Jones Hotel on North College Street. It was built in the mid-1850s as a residence for the dentist, F. G. McElhaney, who in 1860 added to the house at the rear and ran it as a hotel. It, too, is in typical Greek Revival style, with striking detail on the fluted portico columns and other parts of the large structure, both inside and out.

Top, McElhaney House
Bottom, Moore-Whatley House

The preceding three lost Greek Revival style houses recorded by HABS were town houses. The **Moore-Whatley House**, southeast of the town, was the center of a large plantation of 16,000 acres, according to the late Mrs. Alma Whatley. The house was built about 1840 by Orin Moore, with one story and in a simple style, though with uncommon shiplap siding on the front porch. Once a covered passage connected a dining room to the house. A separate kitchen stood nearby. After the Civil War, the plantation and house gradually fell into ruin. It was razed in the 1960s, by then a piece of simple grandeur amid deserted cotton fields.

Although HABS recorded only four now lost Auburn antebellum houses, one other that was not so recorded, has been lost. The Bondurant-Hare House on South College Street was demolished in 1958 to make room for the development of student apartments. The house, originally of one story, was built in the 1840s by Alexander Bondurant, one of whose daughters married a Hare.

White-Harris House. At least six other known antebellum, Greek Revival houses once stood in Auburn and have been relocated from their original sites, chiefly to avoid the encroachment of new urban development. All of these have been renovated, some according to type, others almost beyond recognition.

The largest and most resplendent of these houses, and the one most elaborately restored, is now known as the White-Harris House. Built in the mid-1850s by James F. White, its original location was on Warrior Court, a short side-street off Bragg Avenue. Since construction, it had so many owners it was familiarly known as "the seven-name house: White-Drake-Echols-Newton-Hubbard-Overstreet-Harris." The neighborhood around it became crowded with low-rent development.

A few years ago, it was moved by the John T. Harris family to their property in Cusseta to be used as a family guest house. John T. and Eleanor Harris were mar-

White-Harris House

ried in the house when it was owned by the Newtons. Their six sons, in honor of their parents, moved and renovated the building. It is two-story, in typical Greek Revival style, with a small balcony. Its crowning glory is a mahogany staircase as grand as the one lost in the Drake-Samford House. Preservation purists deplore moving historic structures from their original sites, but this house was saved and returned to its former splendor by relocation. It is now known simply as the White-Harris House after decades of a jumble of owners and renters. Mary Eleanora Reese, in the earliest known history of Auburn, wrote that Thornton and Frank Williams built the house, as well as the 1850 Methodist Church, and other unidentified houses.

Armstrong-Ensminger House. Armstrong Street, the original location of the Armstrong-Ensminger House was named for the home's longtime resident, Confederate Captain Henry Clay Armstrong. An unknown builder constructed the house in the 1850s. Armstrong, who was raised in Notasulga, moved his family into it some time in the 1850s. It remained his permanent home until his death in 1900.

The main house is in traditional Greek Revival style in a one-story iteration. Next to it, to the left in this photograph, and very close, is a small building, probably built later than the main house. It was perhaps used as a law office for Captain Armstrong or even as a cook house, or servants' quarters, although such were usually to the rear of the main residence. Both structures had cellars, an unusual feature for early Alabama. An exterior passageway at the rear of the buildings connected the two structures.

Armstrong-Ensminger House

Armstrong's distinguished career included serving in the Alabama legislature (at one point as speaker of the House), building a successful law practice, and serving as Alabama superintendent of education and on the boards of trustees of Alabama Polytechnic Institute and Tuskegee Institute. The culmination of his public service was his appointment by President Grover Cleveland to be consul general of the United States in Rio de Janeiro, Brazil. His grave in Auburn is marked by the tallest monument in Pine Hill Cemetery, which lies just across the street from his old home place.

Shortly after World War II, the Leonard Ensminger family bought and lived in the house, frequently renting rooms in the smaller building to students. The family moved to Gold Hill in the early 1950s and moved both houses there in 1984, to escape developmental crowding. The small house, rented in Gold Hill for several years, is now vacant and decaying. The main house has been renovated in a manner slightly different from its original exterior style and original center hall, double-pile plan, but retains the Greek Revival look.

Nunn-Winston House. To sidestep the owner's plan to raze it, the Nunn-Winston House, originally located on South Gay Street, was moved to Auburn's Kiesel Park in 1996 with funds raised by the Auburn Heritage Association. The City of Auburn later renovated it and now rents the building for weddings and other occasions. A typical one-story Greek Revival style town house, it is notable for the dentil work just below the eaves. The house, once the home of the Nunn and then the Winston families, was built in the 1850s.

Samuel Nunn was one of Auburn's first settlers and an early trustee of the East Alabama Male College. In 1887, a daughter of Samuel Nunn sold the house to Thomas Harris Winston, a wounded Civil War veteran. Ownership of the house eventually descended to Neva Winston, an unmarried daughter of the Winston family. Miss Neva took in university students as boarders, and the house remained in the family until the 1980s when it was sold to a motel. Removal to Kiesel Park saved it from destruction.

Nunn-Winston House

Steadham-Stewart House. Of unusual configuration, the one-story Greek Revival Steadham-Stewart House originally stood on the Opelika Road. The Danny Blessing family relocated the building to Highway 147 in the mid-1980s. The original four-room section of the house was built in the 1850s, with the usual floor plan of central hall flanked by two rooms on each side.

From 1898 until his death in 1938, Dr. Oliver M. Steadham owned the house, then named "Cedar Villa" for the stately cedar trees lining the walkway from the Opelika Road to the front steps. He bought the house from a little-known Confederate general, George Paul Harrison, who practiced law in Opelika and Auburn following the Civil War. Steadham, originally from Lineville, Alabama, was one of the first physicians to practice in Lee County. He opened a drugstore on North College Street that he later sold to his young assistant, Homer Wright. He also was one of the founders of the Bank of Auburn (now AuburnBank).

Steadham-Stewart House

For many years, the house had an addition to the left that became a rental apartment. A family account has it that as payment for a medical bill, one of Dr. Steadham's patients, a carpenter, built the addition in lieu of settling his bill in cash. The very left of the addition has a gazebo look and was topped by a weathervane that is still owned by the family. The addition (of uncertain date) to the original Greek Revival style house, gave an unusual appearance to the building. After the addition, the main entrance to the house was shifted from the centered front steps at the original part of the home to the steps to the left at the "gazebo."

After Dr. Steadham's death, the house was occupied by his daughter and her husband, Gladys and Glenn Stewart. Upon Mrs. Stewart's death, the house was to

Steadham-Stewart House, after its relocation

be razed to clear a large part of Opelika Road as the site of the present post office. Moved to Highway 147, it was saved from demolition by the Blessings, who extensively renovated it.

Glenn Cottage. The Glenn plantation cottage that stood on Highway 147 was the small, one-story home of the Reverend John Bowles (or perhaps Bowls) Glenn, an early settler of Auburn and the first chairman of the East Alabama Male College board of trustees. A Methodist minister with little formal education, he was a major mover in the founding of the college, which he also served as treasurer. He was succeeded as treasurer by his son and then by his granddaughter, so that for almost one hundred years every check issued by the college was signed by a Glenn.

The house, built probably in the 1850s, originally had two rooms with dog-trot breezeway down the center. It was later added to, though still modest, a small portico and two slender box (square) columns giving it a slight Greek Revival look. In the years after the Glenn family left, the house became a rather shabby rental property. A few years ago, the owner sold the property and planned to raze the house. However, a family that was renovating an old house across the road, stopped the demolition just in time to save the two original rooms, moving them across the road and adding them as a wing to their house, a fortunate adaptive use of the remains of a historic plantation home.

Glenn Cottage

Early Period Houses

Boykin-Guthery House. Another house from the antebellum era, now known as the Boykin-Guthery House, has survived two moves. Wallace Drake built the house in 1851 on North College Street in the area now designated a historic district. The owners moved it in the early 1920s to Bragg Avenue, selling the original site for a new house in a then-fashionable "Spanish" style. Eight decades later, in 2000, to avoid its destruction on Bragg Avenue, Ann Pearson, the mistress of Noble Hall, moved the Boykin-Guthery House to the grounds of that plantation house on Shelton Mill Road.

Boykin-Guthery House

Betty Spooner and children, at their farmhouse in the Auburn area

6

From the Civil War to World Conflict, 1865–1918

The Civil War proved to be extremely costly and very injurious to the "loveliest village." With the Confederate defeat, slave owners lost their financial investment in slavery, and at the same time had to deal with a serious labor shortage. As for the emancipated slaves, the Federal government soon abandoned them and left them friendless. Meanwhile, the Southern financial system had collapsed with the Confederacy, and Auburn's citizens, desperate for credit to help them start over, had no source of funds—just worthless Confederate currency. Consequently, the town's economy remained severely enfeebled long after the close of the war.

The military struggle left many scars. In both 1864 and 1865, Federal troops raided the town, tore up the railroad tracks, burned warehouses, and looted the stores. In between the two raids, in December 1864, a severe tornado killed five people, blocked the streets with fallen trees, and destroyed considerable property, including the Baptist Church and the boyhood home of C. C. Grayson, son of the Confederate postmaster. Describing the town's desolation, he recalled that grass was growing in the streets, stores stood empty and abandoned, and goats were wandering about the streets. In another recollection, Professor Bennett Battle Ross remembered that only one new house was built in the Auburn community in the ten years after the Confederate surrender at Appomattox. In that decade, the paucity of resources affected the accommodations of both the living and the dead. Many prominent townspeople who expired in this economically deprived era could not afford gravestones in Pine Hill Cemetery and consequently lie in unmarked graves.

The population figures for the period register a dismal picture of economic stagnation. According to the census of 1870, the village had a population of 1,018.

Isora Slaughter Cottage

In 1910, forty years later, the town had grown by only ten people a year. For all the misery, bloodshed, and international disruption that the guns of August 1914 initiated, World War I, ironically enough, enabled Auburn finally to return to a semblance of the prosperity that the community had enjoyed before the firing on Fort Sumter in 1861.

The portrait on page 90 of Mrs. Betty Spooner and her family illustrates why photographers are considered to be the most talented artists of nineteenth-century Alabama. Sadly, neither the photographer nor the location of **Mrs. Betty Spooner's Farmhouse** has been identified. Posed with considerable dignity and charm before her tiny farmhouse, Mrs. Spooner and her children exemplify the situation of the small farmer in Auburn and the many difficulties and struggles that rural Alabamians experienced, particularly as the nineteenth century drew to a close. Nevertheless, whatever acute concerns Mrs. Spooner might have encountered, her portrait indicates that she met them with both equanimity and considerable strength.

In the nineteenth century, **Miss Isora Slaughter's Cottage** stood at the present location of Smith Hall and directly opposite Samford Hall. The dilapidated outbuildings in Miss Isora's fenced lot may indicate that she once kept cows on College Street; she certainly was engaged in a small-scale agricultural enterprise of some sort. The frayed gingerbread trim on the porch and its unusual design indicate that her little structure once possessed some picturesque charm. Certainly, it appealed to the romantic nature of the couple who posed there as Romeo and Juliet. On the balcony, Miss Mary Drake in a graceful stance assumes the role of Juliet. The daughter of Dr. John Hodges Drake, and like him a talented musician, she played the violin in the college orchestra and was involved throughout her long life in every musical event of importance in the community. Entreating her from below, her Romeo and husband-to-be, was William "Billy" Askew, perhaps best remembered as the first man in local history to follow, for investment purposes, the capricious trends of the New York stock market, which he supposedly did by means of a ticker-tape machine that he installed in their modest house on Thach Avenue.

Broun-Southall House. Depicted here is perhaps the first house of consequence built in Auburn after the close of the Civil War. It was a structure of architectural importance and significant historical associations. The distinguished president of the college in the late nineteenth century, William LeRoy Broun, purchased the house in the 1880s and made expensive alterations to it. After his death in 1902, his daughter Bessie rented the house to Professor James P. C. Southall. She also left for the Southalls her imposing grand piano in the wide central hall. Professor Southall's rambling memoir, *The Abbots of Old Bellevue*, contains important reminiscences of Auburn in the late nineteenth and early twentieth centuries. He and his wife took special pride in the house, in the flower

Broun-Southall House

garden they cultivated around it, and in a partially underground greenhouse that at one time a neighborhood cow fell into. Furthermore, in his memoir, Southall asserts emphatically that Gay Street was the most fashionable residential area in the Auburn of the early twentieth century.

While President Broun lived there, a fire across the street spread to his house, but about fifty volunteers, largely students, were able to extinguish the flames with water from the Brouns' well and from an artesian well that was situated near the southeast intersection of today's College and Thach. Although the volunteers rescued the house, they did considerable damage to the Broun family's furniture in the process. As Mollie Hollifield explained in her history of the village, volunteer firemen sometimes carried a feather bed out the front door, but pitched a marble top table out the window. In this instance, as a direct result of President Broun's experience, the town in 1895 for the first time organized the bucket and fire brigade to more closely regulate and improve the efforts of the volunteer firemen.

After the Broun family sold the house, subsequent owners denuded it by removing its elaborate Victorian trim and boarding over the arched windows in its gables. It served briefly as a fraternity house and was acquired eventually by the Presbyterian Church, which used it for a time as the quarters of the Westminster Fellowship. In due course, however, the church demolished the house and replaced it with a parking lot.

Nathaniel Lupton House. Like the Broun-Southall House, the Nathaniel Lupton House had distinguished architecture and very important historic associations. Since the college and the community little remember Professor Lupton and his remarkable family, it seems appropriate to mention some of their accomplishments.

A chemist, Lupton adopted the new German scientific method while studying at the University of Heidelberg under the guidance of Professor R. W. Bunsen, the inventor of the Bunsen burner. An amateur archeologist, Lupton later conducted the first scientific survey of Alabama's Moundville site. The important record of his work and some of the artifacts he uncovered are housed today in the Smithsonian Institution. Lupton served briefly as president of the University of Alabama where he was popular with the faculty and students, but the continual interference of the trustees in his decisions led him to resign. He came to Auburn as state chemist and professor in 1885 and built on the northwest corner of Gay and Magnolia one of the most significant Victorian houses in the

Lupton House

village, which was particularly noted for its rose garden.

Ella Lupton shared many of her husband's intellectual concerns. Their daughter Kate was the first female graduate of Vanderbilt University, and the couple strongly encouraged President Broun to admit women to Auburn in 1892. The Luptons also cheered another important event in Auburn in 1892. Their son, Frank, was captain of Auburn's first football team, and the Luptons joined Professor George Petrie, the coach, in paying for the team's uniforms. Frank, who eventually studied medicine at the Johns Hopkins University and became a distinguished Birmingham surgeon, always regretted that he made only the second touchdown in the college record book, but he did kick the first field goal in Auburn's football history. The Luptons' second daughter, also named Ella, married General Robert E. Noble, an Auburn graduate from Anniston, who had a long notable career as a surgeon in the U.S. Army. He won particular distinction and many medals and commendations for his service in World War I.

Professor and Mrs. Lupton organized Auburn's Conversation Club, which was named in honor of the professor after his death in 1893. Mollie Hollifield, the village historian, has written that "No association of men and women has ever made so unique a contribution to the cultural life of Auburn as the N. T. Lupton Conversation Club." The club had some lively conversations indeed, particularly when Mrs. W. E. Hinds discussed "Women's Suffrage" or after Dr. Charles Cary, a veterinarian with wide-ranging intellectual interests, presented a paper on the poetry of Walt Whitman and the fiction of Stephen Crane. According to a newspaper account, Crane's novels caused an uproar in the Conversation Club. Mrs. Lupton died in 1906, and she and her husband and their daughter Kate lie buried in Pine Hill Cemetery. Kate had a promising career as a professor at Longwood College in Virginia but died young. As for the house, the Sigma Nu fraternity rented it for many years.

Glenn House. The Glenn family, so important in Auburn's history, occupied through the years a series of important local houses. The Reverend John Bowles Glenn, who came to Auburn in 1846, first occupied a small Greek Revival farmhouse (see page 88) on today's Highway 14, now rescued from a bulldozer and moved to a new location. After the Civil War, the Glenn family moved to town and rented the Dillard House, then situated on the southwest corner of South College and Thach and now moved to a new location as the home of the Woman's Club. Later in the nineteenth century, however, Emory Glenn built an attractive Victorian house for his wife and ten children. It was situated on a large lot on the

Dillard House with 1880s alterations

east side of North Gay Street. A young neighbor, Mollie Hollifield, remembered it as "a center of rare, open-hearted hospitality" where visitors found "always cordial welcome, stimulating conversation, political discussions, music, fun, and laughter, food and fellowship . . ." In her happy recollection, Miss Mollie wrote that "No home in Auburn meant more to the town." After Emory Glenn's death, the house survived briefly as home to the Sigma Phi Epsilon fraternity, but it was demolished about 1926. On its large lot, extending southward from the southeast corner of North Gay and Glenn, three fraternities—Kappa Sigma, Sigma Phi Epsilon, and Pi Kappa Alpha—built their houses.

Glenn House

Gachet-Terrell House. On the northeast corner of North Gay and Mitcham, on a large lot across the street from the railroad station, once stood a rambling house owned (and probably also built) in the late nineteenth century by Dr. J. E. Gachet, a young dentist. The citizens of early Auburn had special reverence for military titles and sometimes referred to the dentist as Captain Gachet, but his military credentials remain obscure.

Mrs. Terrell's Boarding House

About 1901, Gachet moved his practice to Memphis, Tennessee, where he prospered, and he sold the house in Auburn to the widowed Mrs. Leila Terrell. For many years, she operated there a popular boarding house for students and townspeople. She lived to be more than a hundred years of age and was as remark-

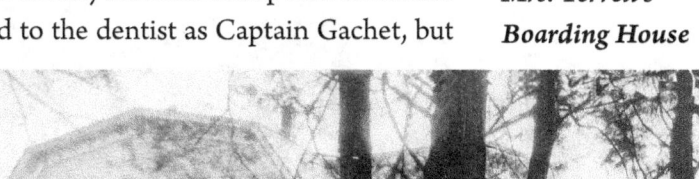

able as the enormous, equally venerable camellia bush that stood in her yard. Mrs. Terrell, her house, and the camellia were Auburn landmarks, now gone but fondly remembered.

Gullatte House. On the west side of South Gay Street once stood the house of Baxter Gullatte, a native of Gold Hill who owned a large grocery store in town and was addressed always as "Judge" Gullatte. A bachelor of Falstaffian proportions, he was noted for his funny stories and infectious laugh. He delighted in twisting words around, and would greet a portly guest by inquiring politely, "How does your corporosity sagasuate this evening?"

As a host, he gave a locally famous 'possum supper that was preceded by a lively cakewalk in which all his guests, young and old, participated. The occasion was reported in the Opelika newspaper and recorded for posterity by one of the guests, Mollie Hollifield, in her history of the village.

Before his house on Gay Street, Gullatte constructed the first sidewalk in the village of Auburn. Many years later the house became the Tea Room, a popular eating place that might have pleased the genial former owner of the structure, who was very fond of Southern cooking. Today a fast food drive-in has replaced the Tea Room and even the historic sidewalk has been eradicated.

Ruins of Gullatte House, destroyed by fire

Whitaker-Tisdale House. Lucius Fletcher Whitaker and his wife Rowena moved from North Carolina to Alabama about 1879; their son, Walter Claiborne Whitaker, earned bachelor's and master's degrees from Auburn and served as rector of the local Episcopal church from 1888 to 1891. A Whitaker daughter married John Jenkins Wilmore of the engineering faculty. The Whitaker residence in its time was considered among the most fashionable houses on then very fashionable Gay Street. Eventually, its ownership passed to Homer Tisdale and his wife Roselle Wright, both noted for their hospitality, their bountiful table, and their bridge parties.

Because several early domestic structures became fraternity houses, photographs of them appear in the college yearbooks. Alas, no readily available information describes their builders or original owners. Prominent among this group is the handsome house in Colonial Revival style that stood on Gay Street at the northeast corner of its intersection with Thach Avenue. A photograph of 1913, when it had become the **Pi Kappa Alpha House**, provides a glimpse of its former grandeur.

Yet another important local structure taken over by fraternities once was situated on a very large lot that stood just to the west of the Lupton House on

*Top: Whitaker-Tisdale House
Bottom: Pi Kappa Alpha House*

From top: Sigma Alpha Epsilon House; Beasley-Bidez House; Friel House

Magnolia Avenue in the middle of downtown Auburn. For many years the Sigma Alpha Epsilon fraternity occupied the house.

Of modified Greek Revival style, but post-bellum construction, the **Beasley-Bidez House** on Magnolia Avenue overlooked Beasley's pasture (on today's Ross Street) where Dr. George Petrie and his compeers laid out Auburn's first golf course. Alice Beasley married Bede Bidez, an enthusiast of Auburn athletics and music. He established his lasting claim to local fame in the Rainbow Division during World War I when he led an army band that crossed the Rhine playing "Touchdown Auburn!"

Friel House, another of an old-fashioned style that apparently dates from the post-bellum era, stood on the north side of West Magnolia Avenue a few houses from the very center of town. It was home to Ercel Thomas Friel of the family that owned the Thomas Hotel.

Bragg House. Tom Bragg, who built this house on the northwest corner of North College and Bragg (a street named for him), taught chemistry at Auburn from 1902 to 1920 and also served from 1913 to 1920 as president of the Auburn Alumni Association. The Alumni Gymnasium served as monument to his popularity with alumni and his skill at fund-raising. In 1920, he left Auburn to begin a successful career with the

Alabama Power Company ultimately serving as both director and vice-president of that enterprise. He nevertheless remained a devoted alumnus of the college at Auburn and a favorite of the local community.

Fullan House. The Michael Thomas Fullan House once stood on the west side of North College Street. It was built in 1907 by a professor of machine design and mechanical drawing who also established the Auburn band. In 1941 the Auburn Alumni Association presented to him a silver loving cup with the following inscription: "Ever remembered with love as one who guided our minds by instruction and made joyful our days with the music of Auburn's first band."

Top: Bragg House
Bottom: Fullan House

Dunstan House and its environs in the early 1900s

Dunstan House. Also in 1907, Arthur St. Charles Dunstan and his wife, Loula Persons, built a house on the west side of North Gay Street very near its intersection with Magnolia Avenue. The son of an itinerant English mining engineer, Dunstan received his early education in electrical engineering at Auburn and did further work at the Johns Hopkins Institute and the University of Chicago. It is not much of an exaggeration to say that he wired the town of Auburn for electricity. He too was honored by the Auburn Alumni Association in 1941 with a loving cup with the following inscription: "Inspiring us as a teacher and holding fast our hearts as a friend."

Duncan House. Dr. Luther Noble Duncan, a leader in Auburn's School of Agriculture and its Extension Service (and eventually a president of the college) built his house on Opelika Road shortly before World War I. It was particularly

Left: Duncan House
Below: Bondurant-Hare House

"modern" in its time because of its porte-cochere.

The **Cliff Hare House** on South Gay Street was especially notable for its architecture and historical associations. Clifford Hare, dean of the School of Chemistry, who played on Auburn's first football team, married into the Bondurant family and remodeled their one-story antebellum house into a handsome two-story

McElhaney House

structure, particularly important for its doorway and fanlight. Similarities to the old college president's home (now Cater Hall) suggest Joseph Hudnut, Auburn's second professor of architecture, as a possible architect for the remodeling. The Hare House was demolished in 1958.

The **McElhaney House** remained the last house still standing in a once-fashionable area of South Gay Street, but it too was doomed. The view (page 115, top) from the site of the Whitaker-Tisdale House shows old Gay Street replaced in the 1970s by penitentiary-style housing surrounded by solid asphalt.

7

Scrapbook of the Late 19th and Early 20th Centuries

Left: J. W. Flanagan House
Above: G. A. Wright House
Below: Meyers House

Above: 149 West Glenn Avenue; Right: Darby-Duggar House, South College Street, present site of AU president's home; Bottom: R. W. Burton's "Four Story" Cottage, East Magnolia Avenue; Inset: Miss Leland Cooper's House, Opelika Road

Top: Miss Mary Cox's House, Cox Street and West Glenn
Bottom: William Crawford Dowdell home, Dovedale, off Opelika Road

Above: Cary Wright House, Corner of North Gay Street and Opelika Road
Right: Pope-Tippins House, North Gay Street
Below: Fletcher Whatley Sr. House, North Ross Street

Top: left, McIntosh-Miller House, South College Street; right, Home Management House, Mell Street. Bottom: Mrs. Tamplin's Boarding House, North Gay Street.

Above: Harvey-Boyd House, East Magnolia Avenue
Right: John M. Thomas House, South College Street

8

Auburn Houses After World War I

As always in Auburn, the growth of the college has been the engine that has driven the expansion of the city. So it was after World War I. Enrollments steadily increased, faculty size grew, new missions in agricultural extension were assigned, and the number and variety of businesses to serve the enlarged community expanded. The demand for housing, usually steady in the 1920s, began to outstrip the supply by the mid-1930s.

From Auburn's early days, houses typically were large buildings on large plots of land. When large properties in the town were divided into spaces for more houses, it was not usually to build in old styles. Few of the newer houses of the 1920s and '30s could properly be said to be comparable with those of the pre-World War I era. No longer were such large houses appropriate for the smaller families growing up in Auburn and depending on very limited incomes during the years of the Great Depression. At the old town limits, neighborhoods of modest bungalows edged northward along Gay Street, outward toward Opelika and Loachapoka, and toward the south and southeast as an era of subdivisions arrived in Auburn in the late 1930s.

The *Lee County Bulletin*, launched in 1937, carefully chronicled Auburn's first great building boom. Paradoxically, it developed during the Great Depression, spurred largely by the availability of building loans through the New Deal's Federal Housing Administration (FHA). The city pushed through or improved streets between old avenues (e.g., Cox, Thomas, and Toomer streets between West Magnolia and West Glenn avenues) opening numbers of new building lots; even more became available with the development of new subdivisions. By 1938, Auburn boasted eight subdivisions: Cary, Cauthen (Woodfield), Cox, Edwards-Irvine (Forest Park), Foster (south along Montgomery Highway), Gardner (Pineview), Pinedale, and Leslie Wright's—only the first few of many to follow.

By this time, city authorities had begun to pay more attention to the growth of

Top row: left, 210 South Gay Street; right, 220 South Gay Street
Middle row: left, 248 South Gay Street; right, 254-258 South Gay Street
Bottom row: left, 260 South Gay Street (Ware House);
right, 276 South Gay Street (modified as a daycare facility)

the city and the requirements of FHA regulations regarding subdivision amenities and transitions between city streets and subdivision roads. Developers of subdivisions were paying more attention to what was built in their new neighborhoods. In cooperation with the city and utility providers, subdivisions offered city amenities to buyers, but often required new homes to conform to minimum square footage and minimum dollar investments in the buildings. In recognition of their somewhat "upscale" ambitions, subdivision houses were less likely to be bungalows; more often they were built in a modest neo-Georgian style, often brick-veneered.

Many of the 1920s- and 1930s-era houses in Auburn still are homes for Auburn families. Many others have become student housing, often because heirs of the original families who built and lived in them have moved to other places or other houses. Regrettably, many of this era have already been lost. The expansion of the Auburn business district and of the university and the development of privately owned student housing complexes have taken many houses of this as well as earlier eras.

No family homes remain along the west side of the 200 block of South Gay Street or on half of the 300 block. On the east side of that street, only one house remains in the 200 block, now rented to students, and nearly half of the eastern 300 block is lost to new construction, principally apartment buildings. South Gay Street between Magnolia and Samford avenues once was a residential street of houses from every period in Auburn history. Many of the homes pictured on pages 112 and 114–115 were built in the 1920s and 1930s and were lost between the 1980s and the present day.

Continuing south along the 300 block of South Gay Street, the first three houses on the west side have been removed, the third being the antebellum Neva Winston House. The first of these became a well-known student rental unit (page 114), known as the "Free James Brown House" for the sign that decorated the front of the building that had been painted as an American flag.

In addition to 306 and 308 South Gay Street and the Neva Winston House at 320, a small outbuilding once stood beside and to the rear of the Winston House, presumably originally housing servants, but later college students. An Auburn University parking lot has supplanted these structures.

320 South Gay Street outbuilding

Above left: 211 South Gay Street (Whitaker-Tisdale House, here as fraternity house)

Above right: 271 South Gay Street

Right: 277 South Gay Street

Inset: before view of 304 South Gay Street

Right: after view of 304 South Gay, the Free James Brown House

The remaining original houses on the west side of South Gay Street in the 300 block are intact with the exception of 342-344, pictured below. This is the house into which the Ellis family moved when first arriving in Auburn in 1934, as recounted in Carolyn Ellis Lipscomb's book, *A Widow's Might*. The house was removed by a motel facing College Street.

Of the homes on the east side of the 300 block of South Gay Street, none

Above: the east side of South Gay Street, viewed from the site of the Whitaker-Tisdale House (top left, facing page; see also pages 99 and 104)

Left: 342-344 South Gay Street

remains. Farthest north on this block was 305, home of the Trammell family, a house with Victorian decoration that perhaps dates it slightly before World War I.

Likewise, another landmark modern home on South Gay Street, built for Professor Tidmore, head of the university's agronomy department, was recently

Right: 305 South Gay Street
Below: Tidmore House

replaced with a church building mimicking the diagonal entrance of the lost house. Among tenants in this house when his widow, Sara Tidmore, rented rooms to students, were Paul Rudolph and Mac Hyman.

AUBURN HOUSES BUILT IN the 1920s, 1930s, and 1940s often followed style trends in the rest of the country, and none was more trendy than the 1922 house built on West Magnolia Avenue for the Sheldon Toomer family. Shel Toomer was, by many accounts, the most prominent citizen of Auburn, a leading businessman, pioneer on the Auburn banking scene, and, of course, the Toomer of Toomer's Corner, the heart of the town. The house was designed by Alabama's most successful architect at the time, Frank Lockwood of Montgomery. In Tudor style with half-timbered upper floor and clipped-gable roof, **Toomer's Chateau**, as Auburnites sometimes referred to it, was a stand-out architectural feature of the western edge of Auburn's downtown.

Another significant house in a prominent Auburn location on South College Street was the house known as **The Terrace**, the home of Zebulon Judd, the

Toomer House

Judd House, The Terrace

J. W. Scott House, later Susan Smith Cottage, South College Street

university's longtime dean of the College of Education. The building, perhaps originally a fraternity house, faced South College Street, though an entrance off the intersection of South College and Miller was often photographed. Though in no way architecturally "high-style," the generous proportions of the house project an air of comfort and hospitality, while the running dormer and screened porch emphasize the practicality of the house. The stone wall below the terrace on which the house sat has been preserved for the fraternity house now standing on the site.

Just down South College Street from the Judd house was another dean's house somewhat more tuned in to popular architectural styles. Dean **J. W. Scott's house** was a Dutch Colonial, a design that enjoyed some popularity in Auburn. The signature gambrel roof of the Dutch Colonial can be seen in many Auburn neighborhoods. In 1940, J. W. Scott, dean of the School of Science and Literature, sold his house, built in 1928, to the university. It became the Susan Smith Cottage, a cooperative residence for women students.

Homes of Auburn faculty built after World War I tended to be modest, though seldom ordinary. An example is the house built for the Fred Allisons just half a block from Toomer's Corner on West Magnolia Avenue. The house, it was said, was built entirely of heart pine. Dr. Allison, a distinguished scientist who at one time was credited with the discovery of two rare earth elements that he named Alabamine and Virginium, chaired the Physics Department for many years before he became dean of the Graduate School. He enjoyed a reputation in the town for a dry wit and an enthusiasm for backyard beekeeping. As the Auburn business district expanded westward along Magnolia Avenue, the **Allison House** was eventually isolated as a domestic space. Anders Bookstore next door wished to expand its facilities and acquired the Allison property, offering to give the house to whoever would move it. When no takers stepped forward, owners of the bookstore razed the house.

Magnolia Avenue to the east was also being transformed in the post–World War II period, not by business establishments, but by church buildings and professional offices and, of course, student apartments, sometimes by transforming former houses into office spaces, sometimes by replacing houses with new buildings. An example of the latter is 324 Magnolia Avenue, the home of the family of G. H. Carlovitz, a longtime professor in the Electrical Engineering Department. A law office building now occupies the site.

Another, and much more old-fashioned, faculty home was that of James G. Watwood of the Civil Engineering Department. The house stood on the south side of East Magnolia Avenue; in later days, it might be said, the house was a remnant of housing modesty between the showy mansion now called Greystone Manor to the east, and a fashionable homage to the French "chateau" to the west. The **Watwood House** disappeared several decades ago to be replaced by undistinguished student apartments.

In a much different mode, another Auburn University professor, James A. Naftel

Top: Allison House, 201 West Magnolia Avenue Middle: Carlovitz House Bottom: Watwood House, 420 East Magnolia Avenue

Top: James Naftel House, Pinedale Drive
Bottom: G. H. Wright House, 320 East Thach Avenue

of the soil chemistry faculty, housed his family in this tasteful Colonial Revival house, designed by Helen Womelsdorf, in the charming Pinedale neighborhood. Lately it has fallen to the whim of an enthusiastic Auburn University alumnus who demolished the house and now resides on the site in McMansion style splendor.

Another loss to the zeal of a developer was the charming home of the Wright family, and notably of G. H. "Monk" Wright, insurance broker, appointee to the Auburn University board of trustees, twice-elected mayor of Auburn, and organizer and president of the First National Bank. Reportedly, purchasers of the property razed the house intending to construct condominiums designed particularly for out-of-towners attending Auburn University football games. It is unclear whether the project failed because neighbors objected or because necessary funding did not materialize. It is, sadly, quite clear that today the property is simply an empty lot.

More Lost Neighborhoods

As is true of streets like South Gay, South College, and East and West Magnolia, the modest houses that spread along many streets from the center of the original town in the twentieth century have gradually been pulled down to be replaced by apartment buildings for students, bank branches, and parking lots. On North Ross Street most family houses are gone and little remembered. In the photograph on the facing page, 316 North Ross Street is one of the few family houses remaining in its block. Below it, a lost North Ross house, number 313 near Harper Avenue on the right, reminds us of what once lined North Ross Street.

From the point at which North Ross intersects Opelika Road, all the houses

From top: 316 North Ross, 313 North Ross, 258 Opelika Road, and 300 Opelika Road

in the block to the west have been removed to accommodate the U.S. Post Office, businesses, and apartment blocks. The Duncan and Steadham-Stewart houses are discussed above, but these others made the whole block visually striking, which the new post office could hardly be said to be.

The residential 200 block of Opelika Road was not the only neighborhood entirely removed from the Auburn streetscape. Another was the south side of the block of Miller Avenue between South Gay and South College streets. Once it faced the side of Dean Judd's semi-grand The Terrace on the west corner of the block and one of the modest South Gay Street houses on the east corner. Today that street is given over to student housing—a large fraternity house and its annex to the west and an apartment block to the east. Where the houses below once stood on the south side of Miller, the university now provides a rather untidy parking lot.

One of the most notorious losses of a neighborhood

Top left: 110 Miller Avenue
Top right: 116 Miller Avenue
Right: 122-124 Miller Avenue
Below: Gosser House, Cedar Crest

is the abandonment of the circular enclave at the end of Cedar Crest Drive. It is a mausoleum of six once sturdy homes, now derelict, including the house Walter Burkhardt designed for the Gosser family. The house was constructed of stones collected by the family from the Chewacla Park area and brought to the Cedar Crest site. The rustic interior featured stone floors, wood-paneled walls, and heavy exposed ceiling beams.

Not greatly lamented are the unkempt rental cottages built by Professor Hess behind his home on the east side of the Cedar Crest Circle, known to the community as Hess's Messes. Only two of these buildings remain, abandoned and moldering.

As the student body of Auburn University has grown, the entire south side of West Glenn Avenue

From top: derelict houses at the end of Cedar Crest Drive

Left: one of Hess's Messes

Above: 138, 140, and 144 West Glenn Avenue

in the 100 and 200 blocks and most of the 300 and 400 blocks has been stripped of the family homes that once lined that side of the street, replaced by an assortment of businesses and apartment blocks catering to students. The small bungalows removed are remembered especially for the somewhat idiosyncratic faces they presented to the street.

Although the Auburn business district once included a number of African American businesses, few houses in the older Auburn city limits were homes to black families other than domestics, none that we know about dating before 1960. On the extension of North Gay Street, along the Loachapoka Highway, and outside the city limits between these two arteries were located numbers of African American homes, but no official records or newspaper reports recorded them so far as is now known.

As Auburn expanded into areas that its African American citizens had of necessity developed as almost entirely black neighborhoods, the exclusively white complexion of the city gradually has become more racially inclusive, at least along some of its edges. Likewise the inclusion of greater numbers of less affluent citizens in Auburn has led the city to develop public housing programs to serve that need in the face of rising real estate values and rental rates. Surprisingly, even some of these homes have been lost.

The Moton Apartments were built in 1952 by the Auburn Housing Authority and were initially reserved for African American tenants—a policy later abandoned. They were named to honor Robert R. Moton, the second president of Tuskegee

Institute. Over the years of their use, the conditions in and around the apartment complex became problematic. A report prepared for the Alabama Historical Commission in 2005 concluded, "Moton is now a dilapidated public housing complex ... that is an eyesore for the community and particularly the surrounding neighborhood. Moton is in desperate need of demolition or partial renovation to provide a more suitable living environment and a better sense of community for residents and the surrounding neighborhood." The Housing Authority closed the complex in 2006. Several of the buildings have been demolished. Those remaining are to be renovated before the project is redeveloped and reopened.

Moton Apartments, 204 Martin Luther King Drive

Top: J. A. Cullars's Planing Mill. Bottom: Chancey's Mill.

9

Businesses

Little reliable information has come down to us about the businesses that served Auburn in its first decades. Auburn's earliest Sanborn Fire Insurance map shows that the downtown business community in 1897 comprised:

    3 butcher shops
    1 cobbler's shop
    1 confectionery
    2 druggists
    7 general stores
    4 grocery stores
    2 hardware stores
    1 hotel
    1 livery stable
    1 restaurant [described as "Negro Restaurant"]
    1 stationery store
    1 millinery and dry goods store

In addition, the town boasted within one half mile of the post office:

    3 cotton gin/grist mills (one combined with a sawmill)
    1 planing mill

All of these businesses eventually succumbed. The last of the buildings they occupied, J. A. Cullars's planing mill, stood somewhat forlornly until 2009 on Samford Avenue, empty but stalwart with a straightforward design that must have suited its function well.

In the north end of Auburn were several businesses for processing area farm and timber products. The smokestack on Chancey's mill explains that without in-town water resources, these enterprises were steam-powered.

In downtown Auburn, early businesses opened in Cullars's general store (to the left in the photograph on the next page) across Main Street (now College) from

Top: Cullars's Store Bottom: North College Street businesses in 1918

Toomer's Corner (at right). The business scene, however, has been ever changing; Cullars replaced his store in 1906 with a brick building (see 1918 photo, below) that was rented from 1909 to 1964 to the Bank of Auburn in the corner space of College and Magnolia, while a barber shop opened in the same building.

Though education is Auburn's "business," the Sanborn inventories over the years show that "business" in its more usual sense developed in Auburn not primarily to serve area cotton production, but to provide goods and services that

made the education business possible and smooth. As businesses have come and gone, Auburn's downtown business buildings have typically lasted through many changes in the kinds of business activities conducted in them. Banks become coffee houses; restaurants become gift shops; theaters become office buildings.

We might suppose that bookstores would be an attractive business opportunity in Auburn. Two that came and went survive photographically. Burton's Bookstore lasted longest and is still fondly remembered, not just for the business itself, but for the family that operated it and their contributions to the life of the community. Burton opened his bookstore, on the right in this view, in 1878. It remained in this same location until rival Johnston & Malone Bookstore bought the business in 1968.

Local memory of the Wright Brothers' Bookstore has largely faded, though this image of it remains. The water tower behind reveals its location on the north side of Magnolia Avenue a few doors east of Toomer's Drug Store.

The date of the building that Toomer's Drug Store occupies today at the corner of College and Magnolia is uncertain (see Logue and Simms), but it hardly resembles the many early photographs of it that have survived. There are no

Top: Main Street, Auburn
Middle: Wright Brothers' Bookstore
Bottom: students at Toomer's Corner

photographs of structures that occupied the site before Toomer took it over.

In the twentieth century, Auburn's first two hotels stood next to one another on the west side of North College Street, just before the roadway begins to slope down toward Glenn Avenue. The McElhaney Hotel (later Jones Hotel) was the earlier, a rambling building, originally a residence to which was added a large structure, the two connected by porches (see page 80). In 1900, competition for the patronage of the traveling public arose next door when the Thomas Hotel opened. This building underwent several modernizations in the sixty years of its life.

As the older traditional hostelries disappeared, Auburn's hotel scene

Top: bird's-eye view of Thomas and McElhaney/ Jones hotels Above: Thomas Hotel in 1900 Right: McElhaney/Jones Hotel, 131 North College

Pitts Hotel

was revived by up-to-date modern accommodations in a daringly different architectural style: the Art Deco style Pitts Hotel occupying nearly half the downtown block on the north side of East Magnolia Avenue. The hotel quickly became a center, not only for tourist accommodation, but also for businesses located in the building, and as a center for local entertaining. Early businesses in the building were the Jane Parrot Dress Shop, J. P. Webb's bookstore, the Jacquiline Beauty Salon, the Terrace Tea Room, and Jim Howard Pitts's real estate and insurance business. Later Messrs. Hutto and Higgins barbered there, and Iverson Caldwell operated a men's clothing store.

The Pitts Hotel gradually lost ground to the traveling public's enchantment with motel accommodation. In 1975, to the dismay of many Auburnites, the building fell to the ambitions of developers and a wrecking ball. Not without some local satisfaction, the developers' plans for new construction proved overly ambitious, and the project collapsed. For many years, the site stood vacant. Today two buildings—the five-story Magnolia Plaza and the two-story Hudson Building—occupy the half block on the south side of East Magnolia Avenue where once the Pitts Hotel and its shops, Grady Loftin's 5 & 10, Waldrop's, and the Kopper Kettle welcomed customers.

Above: Downtown Auburn, 1910

Tourists, newspaper photographers, yearbook editors, preservationists, and local snapshot collectors produced many images of the downtown over the years. Typically their images include lost businesses, as well as some that are still operating. In 1910, a photographer captured a view of Auburn's businesses looking north at Burton's Bookstore on the right toward Toomer's Drugstore at center.

A few years later a parade of college cadets is captured passing Benson's Corner (Burton's Bookstore at extreme right) marching eastward past the post

Below: Town View, Cadets parade past Benson's Corner

office (building with half octagon façade), and a residence at the left belonging to the Hardy family.

The early stages of the Auburn business district as it developed to the present may be seen in a 1920 photograph. Although facades have been drastically altered (some many times over) the bones of many of the buildings shown here are still in place. For example, the face of Flowersmiths with its distinctive top has disappeared though the basic building remains.

Two uncommon photographic efforts preserved valuable images of downtown Auburn businesses. In 1943, Creighton Peet published *The Runaway Train*, an entertainment for his nephew, the son of Auburn's Telfair Peet, longtime director of API's Auburn Players. Photographs accompanying the story include Auburn homes and businesses as the toy train wound its way in and out of them (see next page for three views from this book).

Top: Downtown Auburn 1920 Bottom: Flowersmiths

A second valuable record of Auburn's business district was preserved in the early 1980s as part of an architectural survey of Auburn buildings, under the direction of Luther M. Holt for the Lee County Council of Governments and placed in the files of the Alabama Historical Commission. These long-focus images include many "lost" businesses, as well as many still operating today (see facing page).

Feeding town and gown has proven a risky business opportunity in Auburn. Eateries spring up and disappear at an astonishing rate. The sign for the College Inn reminds us of one restaurant that is little remembered now. The manager of the Inn also ran the Terrace Tea Room in the Pitts Hotel when it first opened.

On the other hand, several lost eateries seem to occupy a secure place in Auburn memory. First among these may be The Grille, so called for its theme displaying prominently the Au-

Left: The "Runaway Train" passing, from top, Loftin's 5 & 10 on East Magnolia; King's Flower Shop and Tiger Cafe on North College; and B. C. Pope's Insurance Agency and College Barber Shop on North College. Above: West side of North College Street.

Businesses

East side of North College Street

Above: North College Street, from the Bank of Auburn to the former location of Bayne's Drug Store (next to the Tiger Theater)

Left: looking west on East Magnolia, past the Village Inn (former Pitts Hotel), past Toomer's Corner and the Bank of Auburn (center)

The Auburn Grille, Kopper Kettle, Roy's Diner

burn automobile and especially its grille. The restaurant, in the former Taylor's Grocery building next to Toomer's Drug Store, was opened in the 1936 by the Gazes brothers, affectionately known to locals as "the Greeks," who continued to operate it into the 1960s. The business was continued by five more owners until 2004 when skyrocketing rents for the building forced its closing. The building remains, lately occupied by one of the street's many gift shops.

A spectacular demise was in store for another Auburn eatery, the popular Kopper Kettle on the northwest corner of Gay and Magnolia. The natural gas explosion that destroyed the undistinguished building in 1978 has a permanent place in Auburn history, for not only did the explosion obliterate the Kopper Kettle, but it also seriously damaged the surrounding structures including the Methodist Church and Bank of Auburn.

A little further from the center of downtown Auburn were two more modest, but popular eating places. Just down the hill on the east side of North College Street, next to the Wright's Drug Store, was Roy's Diner. A block further north on East Glenn Avenue was the often-photographed Doll House, perhaps better known as the Sani-Freeze (and popularly as the Sani-Flush) though in 1939 proprietor Red Meagher had first named it the White Elephant.

Left: Doll House as opened
Right: Doll House as Sani-Freeze

As Auburn developed into a community of townsmen rather than full and part-time farmers, the grocery business developed to supply both restaurants and home kitchens. The 1897 Sanborn map shows four grocery stores in downtown Auburn. Into the twentieth century, customers took their grocery lists to Wild Brothers Grocery, Taylor's Grocery, J. T. Hudson Groceries, S & S Grocery, and others less prominent. Few photographs of early independent grocers are known to survive, but in the period after World War I, when regional grocery companies developed, they opened operations in Auburn and appear in photographs of the main streets. One of the earliest was the Jitney-Jungle located near the Tiger Theater on the west side of North College Street, as pictured on the left in this photograph of an unidentified downtown parade.

Succeeding the Jitney-Jungle in the same building was the Piggly-Wiggly grocery store, and later still the A&P store. Under the management of Milligan Earnest, the A&P proved to be the most successful of these enterprises, moving later to larger quarters in a new office building next to the Episcopal Church on Magnolia Avenue that it shared with Markle's Drug Store. Later still the A&P moved to a yet larger

Jitney-Jungle and Tiger Theater

building on South Gay Street next to Dr. Thomas's office. Its final home was a now-demolished building on North Gay Street, the site of today's BB&T bank that acquired it when Colonial Bank collapsed.

Downtown Auburn now has no grocery stores—neither independent nor chain—for they all have moved to set up businesses on the outskirts of town, with varying degrees of success.

The early custom of acquiring at least some foodstuffs for Auburn's kitchens from the surrounding agricultural area was briefly revived in the form of the Auburn Curb Market. To judge from the attention it received from the local newspaper, the Auburn Curb Market must have been an important community asset. At one time, the market was an open-air affair conducted literally at the curb next to the Magnolia Avenue side of the Bank of Auburn building. Later the market was held on the southeast corner of North Gay and East Glenn, and still later behind the city hall on North Gay. The market finally occupied a conventional retail site facing Thach Avenue next to the old Presbyterian Church cum Y-Hut. Built in 1941 with Kiwanis Club funds on university land, it opened at an inauspicious time. Five months after the market opening, the United States entered World War II. Farm labor shortages, Victory Gardens in many back yards, and the public's focus of attention on the war effort doomed the enterprise. The fate of the building is not recorded.

Top: Auburn Curb Market in 1928
Bottom: in 1941

TWO DRUGGISTS APPEARED ON the list of Auburn's earliest businesses, but few details about them are recorded. Before the appearance of national chain drugstores and pharmacy departments in grocery stores and big-box retailers, Auburn had settled down to four oldtime establishments to be joined by a fifth in the 1940s—all local, independent businesses.

Toomer's, of course, was the oldest and still operates today at the same location and possibly in the same building in which it began. Today's interior is greatly changed from this early photograph.

Next on the drugstore scene was Lipscomb's (see photo, page 135), again a business that today remains in the same place and same building in which it began in 1922, a few doors down from Toomer's on the same east side of North College Street.

Bayne's Drugstore did not survive as long, even though it had an enviable location next to the Tiger Theater, and at one time had a thriving business catering to patrons waiting for the next show or feeling thirsty afterward.

A relative latecomer to the drugstore scene was Wright's drugstore on the corner of North College and Tichenor. The building, now occupied by Cheeburger-Cheeburger, was designed by W. N. Womelsdorf as a drugstore entered from College Street and a bus terminal entered on Tichenor Avenue. At one time a high canopy was attached to its north side to shelter arriving buses and their passengers.

Top: Toomer's Drugstore Early Interior
Bottom: partial view of Bayne's Drug Store next to Tiger Theater

When the A&P store moved to the new retail block next to the Episcopal Church on East Magnolia Avenue, C. C. Markle opened his new drug store beside the A&P in the same building. The building itself was unremarkable. With many alterations, it still is in place. Markle's proved a popular hangout for students, both college and high school. A branch was opened in the Southside Shopping Center. Ultimately the business moved, perhaps because space was too limited, to a larger store in Auburn's first suburban shopping center, Glenndean. The business closed in the 1990s.

Though these establishments were built around supplying prescription and over-the-counter medicines, their soda fountains were mainstays of the drugstore business. In that, another establishment, Benson's Confectionery, competed with them. The building originally designated Benson's Corner (in competition with

Markle's Drug Store, East Magnolia Avenue

Left: Benson's Confectionary, Interior
Below: Polly-Tek Shop

Toomer's Corner across the street) was renovated in the 1930s under the supervision of Professor Burkhardt, providing an updated retail space for Burton's Bookstore, a marble front for the new First National Bank, both facing College Street, and another space for Benson's Confectionery facing Magnolia Avenue.

Just as the grocery businesses had moved from downtown to suburban locations, those that had clothed Auburnites began to follow them to the strip malls that sprang up around the town. The general stores then ready-to-wear shops moved out. For ladies, no more Jane Parrot Dress Shop, or Parker's, or Thrasher-Wright, or Polly-Tek.

For men, Iverson Caldwell's Pitts Hotel shop folded with his death; Harwell's on Thach Avenue disappeared, and, holding on until the twenty-first century, finally Olin L. Hill's Menswear was gone. Hill, something of an advertising genius, and still remembered as "The Man with the Tape," was the final iteration of one of Auburn's earliest ready-to-wear businesses. In the same location on the east side of North College

Street, in succession were: T. A. Flanagan's Men's Clothing Store (established in 1855), William David Gilson's Men's Clothing Store, Ward's Men's Wear, and finally Olin L. Hill.

A RELATED AND MEMORABLE Auburn business was Young's Laundry. It first operated from a building designated on a 1928 Sanborn map as "Young's Dyeing & Cleaning Works & Ideal Laundry" on the North side of West Glenn Avenue, where Toomer intersects Glenn. Later, customers patronized Young's at a building facing west on North College Street, next to the railroad tracks. The laundry occupied no architecturally significant building, for which reason, presumably, we have found no photographs of it save this one taken mid-demolition, a scene too often replayed in Auburn's built landscape. Auburn roller skating rink once occupied the building just to the right of the laundry.

Above: T. A. Flanagan's Men's Clothing Store
Below: Demolition of Young's Laundry

10

Movie Theaters

Long before the downtown business section of Auburn came to be dominated by fast-food shops, entertainment businesses were a major draw to the center of Auburn. At times, Auburn offered a roller skating rink, a bowling alley, and at least two pool halls. But the principal entertainment over the years has been movies.

College-sponsored picture shows in Langdon Hall date from 1912, but the first commercial motion picture theater opened in Auburn in 1926. In the years since then, the town has lost six movie theater screens; today none is to be found in the city proper. This is not merely a commercial loss in a business world. Movies are more than a screen and projector; they are the silver-toned projection of our ephemeral hopes and dreams. They go beyond popcorn and a Coke into the land of "wannabe." Whether a slapstick comedy, drawing room drama, musical, or western in the past or an action film, fantasy, sci-fi, chick flick, or adult drama today—movies have been a part of the communal experience that binds a town like Auburn together.

Foreman Rogers opened the first commercial picture show (as the business was once called, rather than movie house or multiplex) in Auburn in an old storefront on North College Street, where a bank now stands. From 1926 until 1928, this first Tiger Theater showed movies featuring such legendary stars as W. C. Fields and Douglas Fairbanks. Its great distinction was that it was the site of the premiere of *Stark Love*, the movie in which Fob James Sr. had the lead role. It ran September 21–22, 1927. Admission was 35 cents for adults and 15 cents for children. Although New York's Museum of Modern Art holds a copy of the film, no image of the original Tiger Theater has been found.

Within two years of the first theater's demise in 1928, the Thomas family, owners of the Thomas Hotel, built the second Tiger, to the south, as a movie palace, or what passed for one in a small town. The cost was $60,000; the architect was

Above: **Tiger Theater**
Right: its original interior

David O. Whillen. The theater was located in the "pebble building" adjacent to the Thomas Hotel with Foreman Rogers as manager, succeeded in time by the still-remembered, longtime manager Gus Coats.

The 715-seat theater, even larger than Langdon Hall, was known for its colorful pennants lining the walls representing the colleges of the old Southeastern Conference. In the 1950s, it was known for the plaster hand casts in the lobby of well-known football players from the era. For a few years, the Tiger gave a trophy to the college football player it considered the most outstanding of the year.

The Tiger was not only a movie palace, but it also had a family atmosphere. The ticket-takers took a personal interest in their customers, especially the small children. Mrs. Tom Sparrow was known for letting in young Auburnites at no charge if the last movie of the evening was halfway through. Occasionally she even did a little impromptu babysitting. One student couple brought their daughter with them in a stroller, and Mrs. Sparrow offered to watch the baby in the lobby while the parents enjoyed the movie. Another favorite ticket-tearer was Mrs. Hoyt Jolly, who moonlighted from her job as hostess for the student activities center in the basement of Langdon Hall.

The Tiger also offered more than movies on its silver screen; it reached out to the community with various events. Before the advent of television, the Tiger screen turned into an imitation football field during out-of-town games. A large board marked off like a field was placed on the stage, and as the radio announcer gave the plays, a volunteer moved an imitation football to the proper place on the lined board.

Early on, the Tiger sold popcorn, but not soft drinks. If one wanted to wash down the heavily salted corn, one had to step next door to Bayne's Drug Store to get a Coke—the fountain, syrupy version that came in a cone-shaped paper cup. Initially, admission to the show was 25 cents for adults and 10 cents for children. The popcorn cost 10 cents and (when later available) the Coke 5 cents, so a child could spend a happy afternoon on the town for the magnificent sum of a quarter (and this included double features!). The Tiger also offered serials (*Captain Video* was a favorite), cartoons, and newsreels for the price of admission.

The Tiger Theater lasted for 56 years, hosting all the great movies of the half century—*The Wizard of Oz, Gone with the Wind*, and the longest-running one (ten weeks), *Star Wars*. By the time it closed on April 26, 1984, admission was

$4 for adults and $2 for children. With its demise, one of the most-loved centers of Auburn social life was lost.

In 1940, however, the demand for motion picture entertainment appeared to be great enough to build a second downtown theater. The Alabama Theaters Corporation announced plans to build on a site next to the First National Bank Building on the south side of Magnolia Avenue, because Auburn, it said, "is deemed to need increased theater facilities." A Montgomery architect, William J. Okel, had been chosen to design the one-story theater. However, the history of this facility falls into the timing-is-everything category. In six months, the United States was at war. A reduced student population and the distractions of war undermined any business rationale for another movie house. Thus the introduction of a second theater had to wait until post-war tastes for movies provided another opportunity.

Long before the Tiger showed its last reel in 1984, it had acquired commercial competition within a block of its ticket booth from two other theaters: the War Eagle Theater and the Village Theater. The War Eagle, located on the corner of West Magnolia and Wright, opened August 19, 1948, on Thomas property, but was built by an out-of-town company and was Auburn's first chain theater, a Martin

War Eagle Theater

movie house. The first manager was Charles Flowers, and a frequent ticket-taker was Crow Wright, a tall, genial man, known for his sporty bow ties, but not for babysitting.

The War Eagle was another small-town attempt at a movie palace. It offered air-conditioning, a high, domed ceiling, and seven hundred leather upholstered seats, as well as all-new sound equipment and a 15x19-foot screen. The company that built the theatre also built Athey's Cafe, which occupied the front of the building.

On August 19, 1948, the War Eagle opened with *The Pirate*, starring Judy Garland and Gene Kelly. By that time, local admission prices had risen to 32 cents for adults and 25 cents for children. The high point of the War Eagle's thirty-seven-year existence, was a movie premiere. In October 1970, the theater hosted the state's first showing of *I Walk the Line*, based on Madison Jones's novel, *An Exile*. Jones, writer-in-residence at the university, was on hand to greet a large crowd of admirers. Johnny Cash, of course, sang the theme song. Following the showing, a large party was held in the old Athey's Cafe. Its showpiece was a champagne fountain, something new to small-town moviegoers and put to considerable use! The War Eagle Theater closed in 1985, only a year after the Tiger.

War Eagle Theater Marquee

In May 1969, another chain movie house, the Village Theater, opened on South Gay Street. The Village was part of the Plitt chain, which the Tiger had also been since 1978. Unfortunately, images of the building as a theater are rare and only distance shots.

A 700-seat theatre, it had none of the original style of the two older theaters. According to the manager, Beth Peak, the Village was "twinned" in April 1984. This divided the theater into two 350-seat auditoriums, offering two different features at the same time. The longest run of a movie in the Village, Peak remembers, was *Terms of Endearment* at ten weeks. *Superman* was a close second. These films were then moved over to the Tiger, a member of the Plitt chain by then, where they had further record-breaking runs. The highlight of the Village's sixteen years was also a premiere. *Norma Rae*, filmed mostly in Opelika and starring Sally Field, had its state premiere at the Village in the early 1980s. Field, who did not appear at the premiere, later won an Oscar for best actress for her title role. There was no party with champagne following the showing; movie houses as well as premieres had scaled back considerably.

The Village Theater was also the victim of an explosive event on January 15, 1978, when the disastrous Kopper Kettle explosion occurred. Located diagonally across the intersection from the explosion site, the theater sustained partial damage. Coincidentally, the movie playing was *Close Encounters of the Third Kind*.

On September 26, 1985, the Village Theater went the way of the Tiger and the War Eagle. It ran its last double reels, and sold out to its neighbor, AuburnBank. With its closing, no theaters were left in downtown Auburn. Multiple-screen theaters had replaced them out on Opelika Road, and the half-century tenure of the old downtown movies was lost to time and technology.

Unlike many cities and towns in the Jim Crow South, Auburn theaters did not accommodate African American patrons with

Above: Village Theater Marquee
Right: Samuels' Theater Building

separate entrances and balcony seating, although Opelika's Martin Theater did. Unusually for a town of Auburn's size, there were theaters operated exclusively for black moviegoers.

According to *Lest We Forget,* a recently published volume that African Americans in Auburn have written about their history, a movie theater in a black neighborhood was opened by Philip Foster and Otis Adams around 1944. It was succeeded by Samuels' Theater on White Street, which was opened by the Samuel brothers in 1946. The photograph is a view of the building after abandonment and shortly before demolition in 1986.

Reportedly, the most popular attractions at Samuels' Theater were musicals and cowboys-and-Indians movies during which audible audience approval greeted Indian successes. The only motion picture that former patrons recall by name was *Imitation of Life,* the Hollywood account of racial "passing," either the 1934 version starring Claudette Colbert and Louise Beavers or the 1959 remake of the movie featuring Lana Turner and Juanita Moore.

Though not literally in Auburn, the Auburn-Opelika Drive-In Theater was once an important part of the movie scene. The business opened in 1951 on what is now the corner of Opelika Road and University Drive with space for three hundred cars. After many successful seasons, its patronage began to dwindle as motion picture attendance declined nationwide. The drive-in closed in 1977. The screen and the rows of window-hung loudspeakers were removed shortly thereafter and the property was redeveloped as a strip mall.

Pop Raines's Beverage Shack

11

Another Entertaining Business

Until the late 1960s, alcohol could not be purchased or served within the Auburn city limits, so places that sold beer, even with a full meal, had to be located beyond the city limits. Consequently, the popular beer buying/consuming businesses were usually located on Opelika Road and Highway 29 South just beyond the city limits. With its large student population, Auburn has had its share of beer joints over the years. Some of the most well-known ones have been lost, in many cases because of their location at some distance from downtown and the campus.

One of the best-known beer joints in the late 1950s and the 1960s was Pop Raines's Beverage Shack on Highway 29 South, to the east, located at the top of a slope in an old cow pasture, on property owned by the Pace family. Herschel "Pop" Raines turned the rickety building, once a tenant shack, into a thriving beer joint. The business doubled as his home—the entire family of Mr. and Mrs. Raines and several children lived in cramped quarters behind the front counter of the beer paradise.

To reach the shack and buy a cold one, customers passed through a gate that led to the big field, where beer business was transacted in a front office mainly held together by old tin beer signs and colorful beer packaging. Consequently, loyal customers dubbed it the Cornfield Country Club. The bar sat at an angle in a corner and above it a sign in large letters proclaimed "NO PROFANITY ALLOWED." Pop was known to keep a shotgun behind the front counter in case anyone did not follow the dictates of the sign, or caused any other disruption while swilling his product.

One patron remembers that behind the shack (and the family quarters) was the biggest stack of old beer cans he had ever seen (a modern recycler's dream!), at least four feet high and a hundred feet long, the result of Pop's idea of cleaning up after customers who drank at the bar instead of buying a take-out.

Pop and his shack disappeared sometime in the late 1960s, and some have complained that beer never tasted the same consumed in downtown comfort rather than in the Cornfield Country Club.

An earlier beer joint that was closer to campus was the distinctive-looking Windmill. Its windmill blades actually rotated so that, generally speaking, it looked like a real windmill, though it was actually a filling station. It was located on Opelika Road (Highway 29 East), west of its intersection with Dean Road, just outside the city limit at the time. Opened in the 1930s and closing in the 1950s, the Windmill featured a pot-bellied stove and a few booths in its one big room.

Below: The Windmill
Bottom: The Casino

The establishment was especially popular with World War II veterans who liked to gather there, have a few bottles of the going product, and swap war stories.

Despite its amusing resemblance to a windmill and legitimate function as a filling station, the Windmill had a shady side. It was known for selling beer to underage students back when there were no student ID cards or other standard forms of age identification. Also, back in the 1930s, a grand jury indicted the owner for running a

"disorderly house," after a shooting on the premises. This poor publicity ran on the front page of the *Lee County Bulletin*, but the Windmill endured until well after the fracas.

BEYOND SOUTH COLLEGE STREET at the time, on the Montgomery Highway, Everett Harwell opened the Casino in 1948, offering favorite beverages and a large dance floor to college students and occasionally to mature-looking high schoolers.

Big Blue, Harry's, and The Tiger

The joint known as Big Blue occupied a former service station of faintly Style Moderne design.

A number of other establishments of the same character were scattered beyond the city limits, just beyond the reach of Auburn's vigilant bluenoses—establishments like Beauty Rest Motel, Archie's, Midway Tavern, and The Tiger.

Second Auburn Post Office, left foreground (see also page 132)

12

Public Buildings

According to Mary Eleanora Reese's history of the village, a post office was Auburn's first public building. Like the first houses and early churches of the settlement, it was constructed of logs. It was situated across the village's main street from where the University Chapel now stands. The federal government chartered it with a fourth-class rating on June 15, 1839. As a Confederate facility during the Civil War, the Auburn post office proved a convenient target for Federal cavalrymen who tore up and looted it during their hit-and-run raid on Auburn in July 1864.

The earliest public building for which a documentary visual record exists, is the post office that was included on the 1897 Sanborn Fire Insurance Map of Auburn. That building faced College Street (then called Main Street) next to the Benson Building across from the college campus. By 1909, the post office had moved around the corner and stood next to the east end of Benson's, facing today's Magnolia Avenue. A number of early photographs show glimpses of this distinctive building with its half-octagon façade.

By 1919, the Auburn post office served the public from a building on North College Street, directly across the street from the McElhaney Hotel. Finally, in 1939, the U.S. Postal Service moved into a handsome new facility on Tichenor Avenue, built as a government project and featuring a stylized eagle carved into the arch over its east entrance. When the City of Auburn later acquired the building for its city hall, the fittings in its public lobby were replaced, but the important structure itself very auspiciously survives.

From its earliest history the village of Auburn had zealous fire-fighting volunteers who participated in what were called bucket brigades, but they had neither organization nor equipment sufficient to address the problems they faced. A fire in 1893 severely damaged the business district and was quenched only by a fortunate rainstorm. By the early twentieth century, however, led by Albert Thomas, the citizenry organized a more efficient volunteer group. Its first small fire engine was housed in the space, just east of Toomer's Drugs, where Tamplin Hardware operated for many years. A well at Toomer's Corner and another at Thach and College provided a source of water.

The provision of public services had changed dramatically by 1928. The city's property on the south side of Tichenor Avenue, once used for schools, in time became the site of the Auburn Telephone Exchange, a printing company, and, by 1937, business offices for the *Lee County Bulletin*. In 1928, city offices moved into a storefront at 111 East Magnolia Avenue. That building housed not only the city government, but also the fire department, and, incredibly enough, the town jail. The fire engine was stowed behind the building underneath the town's water tank. By 1931, however, city officials were able to move into the picturesque combination town hall, fire station, and firemen's dormitory pictured below on North Gay Street. The city jail and police department were located to the rear of this complex.

When the new public school opened on Samford Avenue in 1931, the old

Auburn Town Hall and Fire Station

Public Buildings

Left: Auburn Public Library
Below: Scout Hut on 1928 Sanborn Map

Lee County High School on Opelika Road was used, among many varied purposes, as the site of the first, rather pathetic, Auburn public library. Later, with a donation of property next to her North Gay Street home, Mrs. Mollie Hollifield Jones ensured that Auburn would have a real public library facility. Its building is still there, converted to other purposes. Meanwhile, a much larger Auburn public library was built on Ross Street. It in turn has been replaced by today's large complex on the corner of Dean and East Thach.

Facilities for Auburn's scouting activities are semi-private, but of public interest. The original Girl Scout hut on Drake Avenue, designed by Walter Burkhardt, has been preserved and is still used. The first Boy Scout hut appears on the 1928 Sanborn map of Auburn on College Street, about where New Fraternity Row rose in the 1930s and where the Auburn University Hotel and Conference Center now stand. A history of Auburn scouting published in the *Lee County Bulletin*

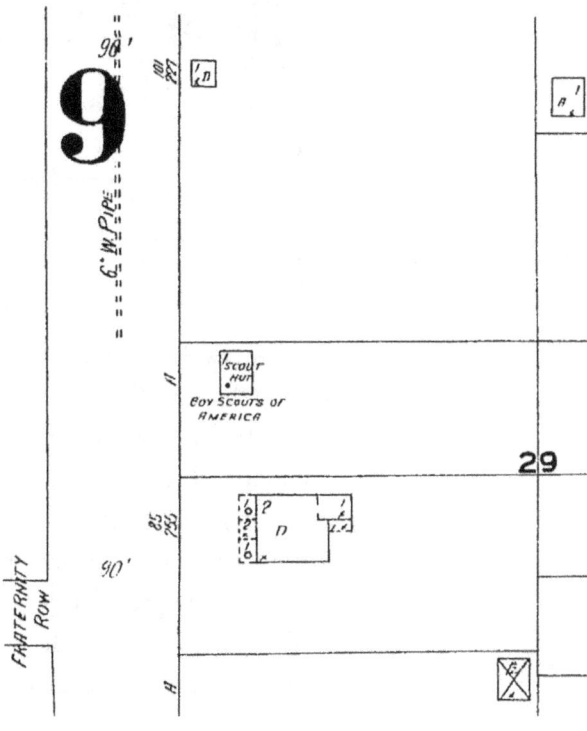

Scout Hut, Architect's Drawing

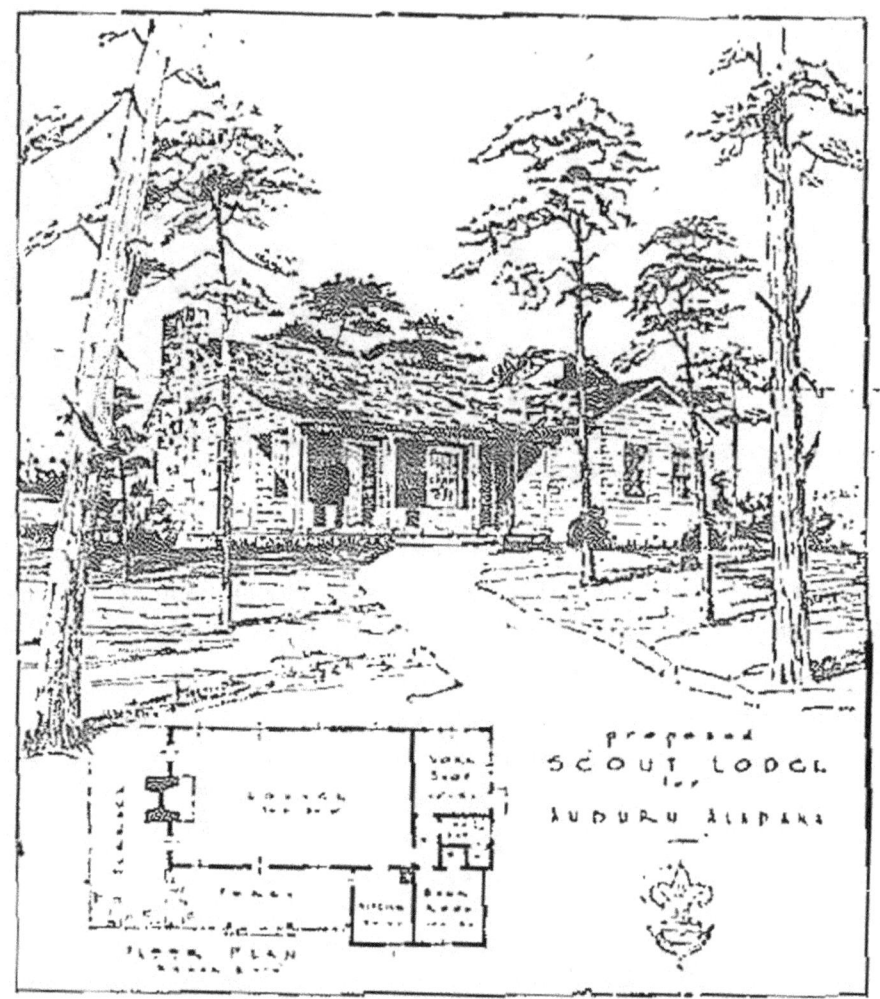

in 1942, explains that "The boys obtained a cabin on the school campus . . . furnished them by the Lions Club."

In 1941, a new, more elaborate Boy Scout lodge, with large meeting space, kitchen, and even living quarters for a scoutmaster was built. The facility, designed by Milton Hill, was constructed by the college's department of buildings and grounds on college property in a wooded area a short distance to the southwest of the college president's home. As the university expanded and room for new buildings was required, the Scout lodge was preserved by moving it to the southeast part of the city surrounded by residential properties on Heard Avenue.

13

Transportation

Transportation as a business came to Auburn early and vigorously. Horses and wagons traveled Auburn streets at the beginning not only on personal errands, but also to bring cotton to the mills in the north end of town, timber to sawmills and planing mills, and sometimes groceries to the back doors of family homes. The earliest buildings associated with transportation were the carriage factory and the railroad depot. In the *Auburn Gazette* of October 8, 1852, Isaac Stelts and Joseph Allan announced the reopening of the Auburn Coach Factory, rebuilt after an earlier fire. The factory is long gone; no image remains to remind us of this early Auburn enterprise.

The first Auburn train station, destroyed by raiders at the end of the Civil War, was replaced by a second located somewhat to the west of the present depot building. A lightning strike is believed to have started the fire that consumed this building.

The building that still stands on the south side of Mitcham Avenue, Auburn's third train station and once the Western Railway of Alabama depot, had seen much better days before the suspension of passenger and freight service to Auburn. Its earlier appearance is not distinctive as railroad depots go, but seems dignified and welcoming when compared to the state of the building in the spring of 2011. Its original impression having been "lost," we include it in the annals of Lost Auburn.

The arrival of the automobile age changed Auburn, as it changed

Second Auburn Train Depot

Third Auburn Train Depot

the world at large. No reliable record of the first automobile on Auburn streets is available, but automobile service stations began to pop up along Auburn streets early on. On North Gay Street in the 1930s, Glenn Stewart's Shell Service Station was supplying gasoline and oil to local motorists.

Stewart's Shell Service Station

*The Bottle
Below: Hatchett's
Service Station*

Although it was not located in Auburn proper, this landmark, The Bottle, a service station of striking appearance north of town, is so fixed in town lore and memory that it deserves a place in this account of lost landmarks. The public could buy fuel, snacks, and from the top of the bottle a view of the surrounding countryside. The structure burned in 1933.

Farther north on Gay Street, at its intersection with Opelika Road, was Hatchett's Service Station. To attract customers, the motorized conical roof revolved, one of Auburn's earliest outdoor advertising gimmicks. Whether from mechanical difficulties or economic neces-

sity, in its later years, the roof stood motionless.

A more modern, and memorable, service station was Chief's Sinclair Station at the corner of North College and Glenn, across the street from the First Baptist Church. (The Baptist pastorium is the building in the lower right corner of this photograph.) "Chief" Shine provided the first rental car service in Auburn, becoming popular with the student population at a time before Auburn students considered an automobile a necessary accessory to college life.

The pioneer Auburn automobile dealer was Anderson Blackburn, who arrived from Opelika in the early 1930s to open the Tiger Motor Company, selling Ford automobiles. Tiger Motors occupied two buildings—one

Top: Chief's Sinclair Station
Above: Tiger Motor Company Sales Office and Service Building
Right: Tiger Motor Company, office interior

Left: Blackburn, Carver, Ford
Below: Tiger Motor Company, North Gay Street

the sales office, the other the service shop—on the northwest corner of Glenn and North College. Blackburn, a significant Ford distributor in the early auto sales industry, traveled to Tuskegee to meet Henry Ford when he stopped there to consult with George Washington Carver. After Blackburn sold the Tiger Motor Company, the business moved to North Gay Street, occupying a building of modern commercial design, also now lost.

One of Tiger Motor Company's competitors was the Martin Motor

Company, whose building replaced Hatchett's Service Station at the Opelika Road-North Gay Street intersection. This business was later removed to make way for the A&P grocery store that, still later, was demolished to provide a site for the grandiose Colonial Bank branch building (now BB&T bank).

Auburn entered the age of air travel cautiously when the Auburn-Opelika airport was opened in 1933. Scheduled commuter service to regional airports in Atlanta and Montgomery was attempted on occasion, but never proved profitable. With substantial financial support from Auburn University, the facility, serving principally private and corporate clients attracted to university functions, has been kept technologically up-to-date. A new terminal building has been completed, facing the old terminal across the airport's main runway. The old terminal, a Walter Burkhardt design, pictured below, was razed, joining the long list of Auburn's lost buildings.

Top: Martin Motor Company
Below: Auburn-Opelika Airport Terminal

14

Peroration

This volume offers a backward glance through Auburn's history.

A series of natural and man-made disasters has destroyed Auburn homes and businesses through the years. At least two powerful tornadoes have struck the town with ruinous damage to persons and property. Fires more than once have devastated the business district. Indeed, throughout the community, flames have destroyed with equal ferocity the homes of rich and poor alike. The Kopper Kettle explosion did extensive harm to the very center of the town, battered a sturdy bank building, and damaged the Methodist Church at a site where its congregation had worshipped, undisturbed, since 1837. During the Civil War, Federal troops twice raided the community and disrupted commerce, tore up railroad tracks, burned buildings, and looted stores and homes, while the war itself left the community bankrupt and poverty stricken in defeat.

Yet, these natural and man-made disasters pale in comparison to what we ourselves have done to the "loveliest village." Our bulldozers have done more damage to the town's character than the combined effects of storms, tornadoes, fires, gas leaks, explosions, and the depredations of Yankee soldiers. Our losses do not stem from an invading army. With Pogo, we realize, "We have met the enemy and it is us!"

Index

Many buildings and businesses in this index are listed under the first letter of the owner's full name, e.g., George Petrie House, not Petrie House, if they are so named in the text.

A

The Abbots of Old Bellevue 93
Acton Court 70
Adams, Otis 149
African Americans 5, 30, 54–58, 69–71, 124–125, 148, 149. *See also* slaves, slavery; *See also* freedmen
agriculture 4, 5, 14, 27, 77, 92
Akron Plan 65, 66
Alabama Agricultural and Mechanical College 7, 10, 26
Alabama Commission on Higher Education 32
Alabama Cooperative Extension System 15, 27, 32, 102
Alabama Federation of Women's Clubs 22
Alabama Historical Commission 125, 133
Alabama Male Institute 68
Alabama Polytechnic Institute 7, 19, 37, 52, 55, 63, 74, 86, 133
Alabama Power Company 101
Alabama, State of 5, 7, 10, 14, 26, 32, 52, 86
Alabama Theaters Corporation 146
Alexander (black teacher) 54
Allan, Joseph 159
Allison, Fred 119
Allison House 119

Alpha Gamma Rho 42, 43
Alpha Lambda Tau 14
Alpha Tau Omega 37, 38, 40
Alumni Gymnasium 28–30, 100
AME Zion Church 54, 56, 70
Anders Bookstore 119
antebellum period 7, 10, 11, 15, 17, 18, 47–49, 61, 77, 78, 79, 80, 81, 82, 83, 84, 89, 103, 113
A&P 137, 140, 164
Archie's 153
Armstrong-Ensminger House 85–86
Armstrong, Henry Clay 85
Armstrong Street 85
Art Deco style 131
Askew, Mary Drake 93
Askew, William "Billy" 93
Athey's Cafe 147
Auburn 3–6, 47, 77, 82, 86, 132
    business district 5, 113, 119, 124, 127–142, 143–149
    council of 51, 52, 54, 55
    declared a city 54
    fire departments 58, 94, 155, 156
    growth of 5–6, 77, 84, 111, 113, 124, 129, 137
    jail 156
    police department 156
    population of 5, 6, 50, 91
    public housing programs 124
    schools of 50–55
Auburn Alumni Association 29, 100, 101, 102
Auburn: A Pictorial History ix
AuburnBank 39, 48, 49, 87, 148
Auburn Baptist Church 4, 63, 91
Auburn Baptist Church (2nd) 63
Auburn Baptist Church (3rd) 63, 64
Auburn Baptist Church (4th) 63, 64
Auburn Church of Christ 71
Auburn City Hall 53, 155, 156
Auburn Coach Factory 159

Auburn Creed 21
Auburn Curb Market 138
Auburn Episcopal Church (1st) 19, 67
Auburn Female Institute 50–51, 52, 53
Auburn Gazette 49, 159
Auburn Grammar School 55
Auburn Grille vii, 136
Auburn Heritage Association 86
Auburn Housing Authority 124
Auburn Masonic Female College 4, 48–49
Auburn Methodist Church 3, 6, 39, 47, 61–63, 73, 79, 136
Auburn-Opelika airport 164
Auburn-Opelika Drive-In Theater 149
Auburn Players Theater 60, 61, 133
Auburn Presbyterian Church 22, 65, 66, 74
Auburn Public Library 72, 157
Auburn Public School 51–52, 156
Auburn Public School for blacks 54–55, 58
Auburn roller skating rink 142
Auburn Telephone Exchange 156
Auburn Unitarian-Universalist Fellowship 61, 70
Auburn University 4, 7–46, 48, 67, 74, 82, 88, 113, 120, 123, 138, 158, 164. *See also* East Alabama Male College; Alabama Polytechnic Institute; Alabama Agricultural and Mechanical College
    admission of women 95
    Archives and Special Collections 19, 48
    band 101
    College of Education 118
    football team viii, 12, 20, 29, 30, 32,

Index

36, 95, 103, 120, 145
Graduate School 119
history department 20
home economics department 20, 49
physics department 119
School of Agriculture 27, 102
School of Architecture 7, 12, 23, 27, 40, 41, 44, 104
School of Chemistry 103
School of Engineering 7, 11, 14, 16, 18, 22, 24, 40, 52, 99, 102, 119
School of Science and Literature 118
Auburn University Chapel 60, 61, 65, 79, 155
Auburn University Hotel and Conference Center 41, 157
Auburn Woman's Club 18
automobile dealers 162–163

B

Bailey, Jack 83
Bank of Auburn 87, 128, 135, 136, 138
Baptists 47, 63–65, 70, 72
barbers 131, 134
Barn viii
baseball 20
basketball viii, 29, 30, 36
Bayne's Drug Store 135, 139, 145
BB&T Bank 138, 164
Beasley-Bidez House 100
Beasley's pasture 100
Beauty Rest Motel 153
beekeeping 119
beer joints and taverns 151–153
Benson Building 155
Benson's Confectionery 141
Benson's Corner 132, 141
Beverage Shack vii, 150, 151–152
Bibb, Sophie Gilmer 4
bicycle clubs, paths 20, 25
Bidez, Alice Beasley 100
Bidez, Bede 100
Big Blue 153
Biggin Hall 15
The Birth of a Nation 29

Blackburn, Anderson 162
Blasingame family 74
Blessing, Danny 87
Bondurant, Alexander 84
Bondurant family 103
Bondurant-Hare House 84, 103
The Bottle 161
bowling 22, 143
Boyd, David French 19
Boyd House 20
Boyd, Leroy Stafford 19
Boykin Grammar School 56
Boykin-Guthery House 89
Boykin Street 69
Boykin Street Elementary School 58
Boy Scout hut 157
Bragg Avenue 54, 84, 89, 100
Bragg House 100, 101
Bragg, Tom 29, 100
Brewster, Sam 32
Broun, Bessie 93
Broun Hall 11–13
Broun-Southall House 93, 94
Broun, William LeRoy 3, 7, 11–12, 19, 74, 93–94
Bruce and Morgan 51
Bryan, William Jennings 38
bucket brigades 94, 155
building regulations 6, 41, 113
Bullard Hall 34
Burkhardt, Mrs. Walter 78
Burkhardt, Walter 31, 68, 69, 78, 83, 123, 141, 157, 164
Burton, R. W. 50
Burton's Bookstore 129, 132, 141
Button, Stephen 9–10, 11

C

Caldwell, Iverson 131, 141
Carlovitz, G. H. 119
Carlovitz House 119
Carnegie, Andrew 12, 67
Carnegie libraries 13, 23, 67
Carpenter Gothic style 67
Carver, George Washington 163
Cary, Charles 96

Cary-Pick House 82
Cary subdivision 111
Cary Woods 6, 19
Cary Wright House 108
Casino viii, 152, 153
Cater Hall 25, 104
Catholics, Catholicism 47, 68–69, 79
Cauthen, Mrs. 82
Cauthen (Woodfield) subdivision 111
Cedar Crest Drive 122, 123
"Cedar Villa" 87
Cedre Villa 5
Chancey's Mill 126, 127
Charles Coleman Thach House 25
Checkers 71
Cheeburger-Cheeburger 139
chemistry buildings and labs 14–15
Chewacla Creek 20, 80
Chewacla School 55
Chewacla State Park 58, 80
Chief's Sinclair Station 162
Christopher and Lizzie Harper Flanagan House 78–79
churches 61–75
Church of the Holy Innocents 67
Church of the Sacred Heart 68
Civil War 4, 6, 10, 11, 17, 18, 19, 26, 49, 50, 73, 77, 80, 83, 86, 87, 91, 93, 96, 155, 159, 165
Clark, H. L. 55
Cliff Hare House 103
Coats, Gus 145
Code of Alabama viii
College Barber Shop 134
College Inn 134
College Street 16, 17, 37, 41, 44, 65, 71, 78, 82, 83, 84, 87, 89, 92, 94, 96, 101, 106, 109, 110, 115, 117, 118, 120, 121, 128, 130, 134, 136, 137, 139, 140, 141, 142, 143, 153, 155, 156, 157, 162
Colonial Bank 138, 164
Colonial Dames 22
Colonial Revival style 73, 99, 120
Columbus Daily Enquirer 54

Comer Hall 12, 27
Commandant's House 28
commercial expansion 6, 41
Confederates, Confederacy 4, 10, 11, 17, 18, 26, 44, 49, 82, 85, 87, 91, 155
Conversation Club 95
Cooper, Leland 50
Cornfield Country Club. *See* Beverage Shack
cotton 77, 83
Cox Street 54, 70, 73, 75, 107, 111
Cox subdivision 111
Creek Indians, Creek Nation 3, 77
Cullars, J. A. 51, 127
Cullars's general store 127, 128
Cullars's Planing Mill 126, 127
Curtis, Elizabeth Thach 27
Curtis, Nathaniel C. 12, 27, 37, 40, 41
Curtis, Nathaniel, Jr. 13, 27
Curtis, Nellie Thach 13
Cusseta 84

D

Daniel Thomas Gray House 27
Danner, Christine B. 14, 30
Darby-Duggar House 106
Darby, John 11, 49
Darby's Prophylactic Fluid 49
Daughters of the American Revolution 22
David French Boyd House 19
Davis, John Eayres 40
Dean Road 73, 152, 157
Deck Houses 33
Deep South 77
Delta Sigma Phi 41, 42
Delta Sigma Phi House 43
developers 6, 73, 113, 120, 131
Dillard House 96
Disciples of Christ 75
Doll House 136, 137
Donahue Drive 69, 70
Donahue, Mike 30
Dowdell, Betty 49
Dowdell, James F. 5, 48
Drake Avenue 81, 157

Drake High School 56, 57
Drake House 16, 17
Drake Infirmary 17, 25
Drake, John Hodges, Jr. 10, 16–17, 28, 82, 93
Drake, John Hodges, Sr. 82
Drake-Samford House viii, 82, 82–83, 83, 85
Drake, Wallace 89
Dramatic Club 37
Draughon, Ralph 32
drugstores 138–140
Dudley, Frank Judson 23
Duncan, George W. 50, 52
Duncan House 102, 103
Duncan, Luther Noble 27, 102
Dunstan, Arthur St. Charles 102
Dunstan House 102
Dunstan, Loula Persons 102
Dutch Colonial style 74, 118

E

Earnest, Milligan 137
East Alabama Male College 4, 5, 7, 8, 10, 26, 48, 49, 62, 86, 88, 132
Ebenezer Baptist Church 54, 55, 61, 70
Edwards-Irvine (Forest Park) subdivision 111
Edwin Reese House 79–81
electricity 16, 102
Ellis family 115
Ensminger, Leonard 86
Episcopal, Episcopalian 67, 73, 99, 138, 140
An Exile 147

F

Faculty Row 16–28
Federal Housing Administration 111
Field, Sally 147
Fine Arts Center 35
Fire-Eaters 4
fires 4, 5, 9, 10–11, 15, 24, 39, 57, 78, 80, 81, 91, 94, 155–156, 159, 161, 165
First Baptist Church 50, 72, 73, 162

pastorium of 73, 162
First National Bank 120, 141, 146
Fisk University 55, 57, 58
Flanagan, Christopher C. 47, 79
Flanagan, Lizzie Taylor Harper 47, 79
Flanagan, T. A. 142
Fleming, Mary Boyd 19
Fleming, Walter Linwood 19
Fletcher Whatley Sr. House 108
Flowers, Charles 147
Flowersmiths 133
The Flush vii
football 19. *See also* Auburn University: football team
Ford, Henry 163
Foster, Philip 149
Foster, Pompey 56
Foster Street 54
Foster subdivision 111
Foy Hall 30
fraternity houses 37–46, 121
Fraternity Row 41–44
Frazier Street 54, 55
freedmen 54
Freedmen's Bureau 54
Free James Brown House 114
French Second Empire style 17
Friel, Ercel Thomas 100
Friel House 100
Fullan House 101
Fullan, Michael Thomas 101

G

Gachet, J. E. 97
Gachet-Terrell House 97
Gardner (Pineview) subdivision 111
G. A. Wright House 105
Gay Street 24, 39, 44, 47, 48, 51, 63, 65, 69, 73, 74, 82, 86, 94, 97, 98, 99, 102, 103, 104, 108, 109, 111, 112, 113, 113–117, 114, 115, 116, 120, 121, 124, 136, 138, 147, 156, 157, 160, 161, 163, 164
Gazes brothers 136
General James Henry Lane House 17–18

Index

George Petrie House 20–21
G. H. Wright House 120
G. I. Bill 6, 32
Giddens, Susie Hughes 56
Gilson's Men's Clothing Store 142
Gilson, William David 142
Girl Scout hut 157
Glenn Avenue 39, 44, 47, 63, 66, 70, 71, 73, 97, 106, 107, 111, 123, 124, 130, 136, 138, 142, 162
Glenn Cottage 88
Glenndean shopping center 140
Glenn, Emory 96
Glenn family town house 44
Glenn House 96
Glenn, John Bowles 4, 88, 96
Gold Hill 86, 98
Goldsmith, Oliver vii, 3
golf 20, 100
Goodwin Band Building 35
Goodwin Music Building 35
Gosser family 123
Gosser House 122
Gothic style 9, 68
Grady Loftin's 5 & 10 131
Graves, Bibb 30
Graves Center 30–32, 34, 35
Graves Center Faculty Apartments 34–35
Graves Center Student Apartments 34
Grayson, C. C. 91
Great Depression 5, 57, 78, 111
Greek Revival style 32, 44, 49, 62, 77, 78, 79, 81, 83, 84, 85, 86, 87, 88, 96, 100
Greystone Manor 119
The Grille 134
grocers 73, 98, 127, 136, 137, 138, 139, 141, 164
Gullatte, Baxter 98
Gullatte House 98
gymnasiums 28–30

H

Hamill, Howard 62
Hamill Memorial Sunday School Building 62
Hardy family 133
Hare, Clifford 103
Hargis Hall 15
Harper Avenue 120
Harper, John J. 3, 5, 47
Harper, Lizzie Taylor 78
Harper, Thomas 78, 79
Harris County, Georgia 3
Harris, Eleanor 84
Harris, John T. 84
Harrison, George Paul 87
Harry's 153
Harvey-Boyd House 110
Harwell, Everett 153
Harwell's 141
Hatchett's Service Station 161, 164
Heard, Annie 50, 52, 55
Heard Avenue 158
Heisman, John 37
Helms, V. C. 58
Hess, Professor 123
Hess's Messes 123
High Victorian style 23
Highway 14 96
Highway 29 151, 152
Highway 147 87, 88
Hilliard, Henry W. 8
Hill, Milton 158
Hill, Olin L. 141
Hinds, Mrs. W. E. 96
Historic American Buildings Survey 31, 49, 78, 83, 84
Holifield, Alsea 25
Holt, Luther M. 133
Home Management House 109
Hornsby Hall 74
Hospital Association 4
hospitals 4, 10, 17, 80
houses, housing 33–37, 77–125
Hudnut, Joseph 25, 63, 104
Hudson, Belas 52
Hudson Building 131
Hutchinson, J. T. 55
Hutto and Higgins barbers 131
Hyman, Mac 117

I

infirmaries 10, 17, 25
influenza epidemic of 1919 17
Isora Slaughter Cottage 92
Italianate style 9, 49
I Walk the Line 147

J

Jackson, Andrew 56
Jackson, Clarence 56
Jacquiline Beauty Salon 131
James, Fob, Sr. 143
James Naftel House 120
Jane Parrot Dress Shop 131, 141
Jitney-Jungle 137
John Jenkins Wilmore House 24
John M. Thomas House 110
Johnston & Malone Bookstore 129
Jolly, Mrs. Hoyt 145
Jones Hotel 80, 83, 130
Jones, Madison 147
Jones, Mollie Hollifield 7, 25, 95, 97, 98, 157
J. P. Webb's bookstore 131
J. T. Hudson Groceries 137
Judd House 118
Judd, Zebulon 117, 121
J. W. Flanagan House 105
J. W. Scott House 118

K

Kandy Kitchen 38
Kappa Alpha 39, 44, 45
Kappa Sigma 39, 40, 44, 45, 97
Kelley, Charles 37, 44
Kiesel Park 86
King's Flower Shop 134
Kiwanis Club 138
Knapp, Bradford 41
Kopper Kettle 6, 131, 136, 148, 165

L

Lakeview Baptist Church 72
Lakeview Subdivision 72
Lambda Chi 37, 44, 45
Lane, James Henry 18, 28

Langdon, Charles 49
Langdon Hall 49, 143, 145
Lee County Bulletin 58, 111, 153, 156, 157
Lee County Council of Governments 133
Lee County High School 52–54, 157
Lee County Training School 55, 56–57, 58
Leek, Mr. 66
Leslie Wright's subdivision 111
Lest We Forget 149
Levi Lee House 15
libraries 12, 19, 20, 23, 67, 72, 157
Life magazine 33
Lions Club 158
Lipscomb, A. A. 48
Lipscomb, Carolyn Ellis 115
Lipscomb's Drugs 139
Little, Charles 51
Little, Sidney Wall 71
Loachapoka 56, 70, 111
Loachapoka Highway 124
Lockwood, Frank 5, 29, 30, 117
Lockwood, "Tubby" 29
Loftin's 5 & 10 134
log buildings 4, 47, 61, 63, 77, 78, 79, 155
Logue, Mickey ix
"The Loveliest Village" 3, 6
Lupton, Ella 95
Lupton, Frank 95
Lupton, Kate 95
Lupton, Nathaniel 94–95

M

MacIntosh & Leek 66
MacIntosh, S. I. 66
Magnolia Avenue 5, 14, 37, 39, 41, 44, 47, 56, 61, 67, 68, 79, 94, 100, 102, 106, 110, 111, 113, 117, 119, 120, 128, 129, 131, 134, 135, 136, 138, 140, 141, 146, 155, 156
Magnolia Dormitory 34
Magnolia Plaza 131
Main Street 5, 16, 127, 129, 155. See *also* College Street
Manning, W. N. 83
map-index of 1893 16, 19, 24, 25
Markle, C. C. 140
Markle's Drug Store vii, 138
Martin Luther King Drive 125
Martin Luther King Jr. Park 57
Martin Motor Company 163, 164
Martin Theater 146, 149
Mary Martin Hall 12, 23, 67
Masonic Order 11, 48, 56
McElhaney, F. G. 83
McElhaney Hotel 130, 155
McElhaney House 83, 104
McElhaney-Jones Hotel 80, 83
McIntosh-Miller House 109
Meagher, C. R. "Red" 53, 137
Melchior, Lauritz 35
Mell, Annie Rebecca 21, 22
Mell, Patrick Hues 21–23, 26, 28
Mell Street 21, 24, 25, 27, 42, 109
Methodist District Parsonage 73
Methodist Episcopal Conference 54
Methodist Founders' Chapel 61
Methodists, Methodism 3, 4, 5, 7, 8, 26, 38, 47, 48, 61–63, 65, 69, 71, 73, 85, 88, 165
Meyers House 105
Midway Tavern 153
Miller Avenue 118, 121, 122
Miller, Lucy O. H. 57
Milton, Alicia 79
Miss Leland Cooper House 106
Miss Mary Cox House 107
Mitcham Avenue 97, 159
Montgomery Advertiser 48, 52, 55
Montgomery Highway 111, 153
Moore, Orin 83
Moore, R. E. 57
Moore-Whatley House 83
Morrill Land Grant College Act 10, 21
Moton Apartments 124, 125
Moton, Robert R. 55, 124
Mrs. Betty Spooner's Farmhouse 92
Mrs. Tamplin's Boarding House 109
Mrs. Terrell's Boarding House 97
Mt. Moriah Church 58
Mt. Moriah School 55, 58–59
Mt. Vernon School 55

N

Naftel, James A. 119
Nathaniel Lupton House 94–95, 99
National Register of Historic Places 49
Neoclassical style 61, 63, 65, 68, 69
Neo-Georgian style 113
Neva Winston House 113
New Deal 5, 30, 111
New Fraternity Row 157
Newton family 85
Nichols Center 13, 14
Noble, Ella Lupton 95
Noble Hall 89
Noble, Robert E. 95
Norma Rae 147
North College Historic District 12
Northside Grammar School 53
Norton, P. M. "Mike" 32
Notasulga 85
Nuclear Science Center 35
Nunn, Samuel 86
Nunn-Winston House 86

O

Oak Bowery Academy 48
Ogletree-Wright-Ivey House 6
Okel, William J. 146
Old Main 8–11, 15, 48
Olin L. Hill's Menswear 141, 142
Opelika 20, 38, 42, 52, 53, 56, 66, 68, 87, 88, 98, 102, 106, 107, 108, 111, 120, 121, 147, 148, 149, 151, 152, 157, 161, 162, 164
Opelika Observer 67
Opelika United Methodist Church 66
Otis Smith House 25–27

P

Pace family 151
Panic of 1837 4, 47

Index

Parker's 141
parking lots 48, 94, 113, 121
Parrish, J. A. "Fessor" 53, 66
parsonages, pastoriums, manses, rectories 73–75
Patrick Hues Mell Jr. House 21–23, 24
Peak, Beth 147
Pearson, Ann 89
Pebble Hill 4, 9
Peet, Creighton 133
Peet, Telfair 133
Perry-Cauthen House 81, 83
Perry Garden Club 82
Perry, Simeon 5, 6, 82
Petrie, George 12, 17, 19, 20–21, 21, 22, 25, 28, 95, 100
Petrie, Mary Lane 20
Phi Delta Theta 37, 39, 40, 41, 43
Piedmont region 3
Piggly-Wiggly 137
Pi Kappa Alpha 44, 97, 99
Pi Kappa Phi 41, 42, 43
Pinedale Drive 120
Pinedale subdivision 111, 120
Pine Hill Cemetery 5, 79, 86, 91, 96
Pitts Hotel 131, 134, 135
Pitts, Jim Howard 131
Pitts's real estate and insurance 131
Plains region 3
Player, W. L. 57, 58
Plitt Theaters 147
Pogo 165
Polly-Tek Shop 141
pool halls 143
Pope, B. C. 134
Pope's Insurance Agency 134
Pope-Tippins House 108
post offices 4, 53, 88, 121, 127, 132, 154, 155
Presbyterian manse 74
Presbyterian, Presbyterianism 55, 60, 61, 65–66, 69, 74, 79, 80, 94, 138
Prestridge, Virginia Williamson 81
Prohibition 38
Prythian Hall 55

public buildings 155–158
Purvis, Thomas 29

Q
Quinn, I. T. 53

R
racial violence 54
railroad 4, 10, 70, 91, 97, 142, 159, 165
Raines, Herschel "Pop" 151–152
Ramsey Hall 14
Reconstruction 30, 54
Reese, Edwin 79–81
Reese, Mary Eleanora 77, 85, 155
Reese-Wright House 80
rental car service 162
Rice, "Gatsy" 5, 79
Rogers, Foreman 143, 145
Rogers, Will 29
roller skating 142, 143
Roosevelt, Franklin D. 30
Rosenwald Foundation schools 54–55, 56, 57, 58
Rosenwald, Julius 55, 59
Ross, Bennett Battle 38, 91
Ross Chemical Laboratory 30
Ross House 38
Ross Street 100, 108, 120, 157
ROTC 14, 28, 29
Rousseau, Lovell 4, 10
Roy's Diner 136
Rudolph, Paul 117
The Runaway Train 133, 134
R. W. Burton Cottage 106

S
Samford Avenue 35, 44, 53, 113, 127, 156
Samford, Caroline Drake 82
Samford Hall viii, 11, 13, 19, 20, 28, 29, 49, 51, 82, 92
Samford, William F. 5
Samford, William James 82
Samuels' Theater 148, 149
Sanborn Fire Insurance maps 70, 127, 128, 137, 142, 155, 157

Sani-Freeze 136
Savannah Tribune 55
Sayre, Zelda 30
School Improvement Society 52
schools 47–59
Scott, J. W. 118
Scott, Nathaniel 4, 48
Scout Hut 158
Screws, E. A. 56
secession 48
segregation 54, 124
service stations 160–162
Sewell Hall 35
Shannon, Strobel and Weaver 72
Shaw, Robert 35
Shelton Mill Road 89
Sigma Alpha Epsilon House 100
Sigma Chi 44, 45
Sigma Nu 42, 43, 96
Sigma Phi Epsilon 44, 45, 97
Simms, Jack ix
Slaton's Academy 48, 50
Slaton, William F. 48
slaves, slavery 3, 4, 10, 26, 62, 77, 82, 91
Smith, Antoinette 27
Smith Hall 92
Smith, Harry Hamilton 16
Smith, Maude Glenn 16
Smith, Otis 26–27, 28–29
Snow, H. S. 56
Southall, James P. C. 17, 93, 94
Southern Baptist Convention 21
South, Mrs. O. P. 53
Southside Shopping Center 140
"Spanish" style 89
Sparks, Chauncey 32
Sparrow, Mrs. Tom 145
Spidle Hall 28
Spooner, Betty 90, 92
Sports Arena 35–36
S & S Grocery 137
Stark Love 143
St. Dunstan's Episcopal College Center 67
Steadham, Oliver M. 87

Steadham-Stewart House 87, 88
Stelts, Isaac 159
Stephenson, Wendell Holmes 21
Stewart, Gladys Steadham 87
Stewart, Glenn 87, 160
Stewart's Shell Service Station 160
St. Luke CME Church 70, 75
St. Martin de Porres Mission 69
St. Michael's Roman Catholic Church 68
Student Activities Building 35
Student Union Building 30
Style Moderne 153
subdivisions 111
Susan Smith Cottage 118
swimming pools 30, 53

T

T. A. Flanagan's Men's Clothing Store 142
Tamplin Hardware 156
Taylor's Grocery 136, 137
Tea Room 98
tennis 20
Terrace Tea Room 131, 134
Terrell, Leila 97
Thach Avenue 16, 17, 19, 21, 25, 54, 65, 67, 69, 73, 93, 94, 96, 99, 120, 138, 141, 156, 157
Thach, Charles C. 13, 25, 27, 28, 41, 55
Thach, Ellen Smith 27
theaters 143–149
The Terrace 117, 118, 121
Thomas, Albert 12, 155
Thomas and Lizzie Taylor Harper House 76, 78
Thomas, B. F. 39, 138
Thomas family 143
Thomas Hall 37
Thomas Hotel 100, 130, 143, 145
Thomas, J. M. 37
Thomas Street 111
Thrasher-Wright 141
Tichenor Avenue 44, 48, 50, 53, 139, 140, 155, 156

Tidmore House 116
Tidmore, Professor 116
Tidmore, Sara 117
The Tiger 153
Tiger Cafe 134
Tiger Motor Company 162–163
Tiger Theater 71, 135, 137, 139, 143–145
Tippins, Mary 80
Tisdale, Homer 99
Tisdale, Roselle Wright 99
Toomer House 117
Toomer's Chateau 117
Toomer's Corner viii, 30, 117, 119, 128, 129, 135, 141, 156
Toomer's Corner oaks viii
Toomer's Drugs 5, 37, 129, 132, 136, 139, 156
Toomer, Sheldon 5, 10, 14, 37, 117
Toomer Street 44, 111, 142
tornado 4, 6, 78, 81, 91
train depots 4, 159, 160
Trammell family 116
transportation 159–164
Tudor style 117
Tuskegee 5, 86, 163
Tuskegee Institute 55, 124

U

United Daughters of the Confederacy 49
University Drive 73, 149
urban development 6, 84
U.S. Census 6
U.S. Navy 6
U.S. Public Housing Administration 33

V

veterans 6, 32, 33, 35, 152
Veterinary Building 14
Victorian style viii, 13, 23, 37, 61, 63, 94, 96, 116
Victory Gardens 138
Village Christian Church 72, 75
Village Inn 135
Village Theater 146, 147–148

Virginia Avenue 81

W

Waldrop's 131
Ward's Men's Wear 142
War Eagle Theater 146–147
Ware House 112
Warren, Knight, and Davis 5, 30, 31, 37, 40, 44
Warren, William T. 37, 40
Warrior Court 84
Washington, Booker T. 55
Watwood House 119
Watwood, James G. 119
Websterian literary society 10, 11
Western Railway of Alabama 159
Westminster Fellowship 94
Westminster House 74, 75
Whale, John G. W. 5
Whatley, Alma 83
Whidby, Mr. 54
Whillen, David O. 145
Whitaker, Lucius Fletcher 99
Whitaker, Rowena 99
Whitaker-Tisdale House 99, 104, 114, 115
Whitaker, Walter Claiborne 99
White-Harris House 80, 84, 85
White, James F. 84
White Street 149
A Widow's Might 115
Wild Brothers Grocery 137
Wilkins, Pauline vii
William Crawford Dowdell House 107
Williams, Frank 85
Williams, Thornton 85
Wilmore, John Jenkins 24, 28, 52, 99
Wilson, James H. 4
Wilson's Raiders 4
Windmill 152
Winston, Neva 86
Winston, Thomas Harris 86
Wire Road 46
Wirt literary society 10
Woman's Club 18, 96

Womelsdorf, Helen 120
Womelsdorf, W. N. 139
World War I 41, 92, 95, 100, 102, 111, 116, 119, 137
World War II 5, 32, 35, 42, 86, 119, 138, 152
Wright Brothers' Bookstore 129
Wright, Crow 147
Wright, G. H. "Monk" 120
Wright, Homer 87
Wright, Leslie 81
Wright's Drug Store 136, 139
Wright's Mill 20, 25
Wright's Mill Road 58, 80
Wright Street 146
Wright, Thomas Oscar 80, 81

Y

Yancey, Mrs. William Lowndes 4
Yancey, Simeon 47
Yancey, William Lowndes 8, 48
YMCA 23, 24
Young's Laundry 142
YWCA 60, 61, 138

www.ingramcontent.com/pod-product-compliance
Lightning Source LLC
Chambersburg PA
CBHW080433190426
43202CB00039B/2972

Lost Auburn

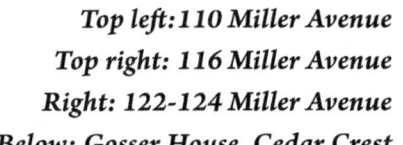

Above: Downtown Auburn, 1910
Below: Town View, Cadets parade past Benson's Corner

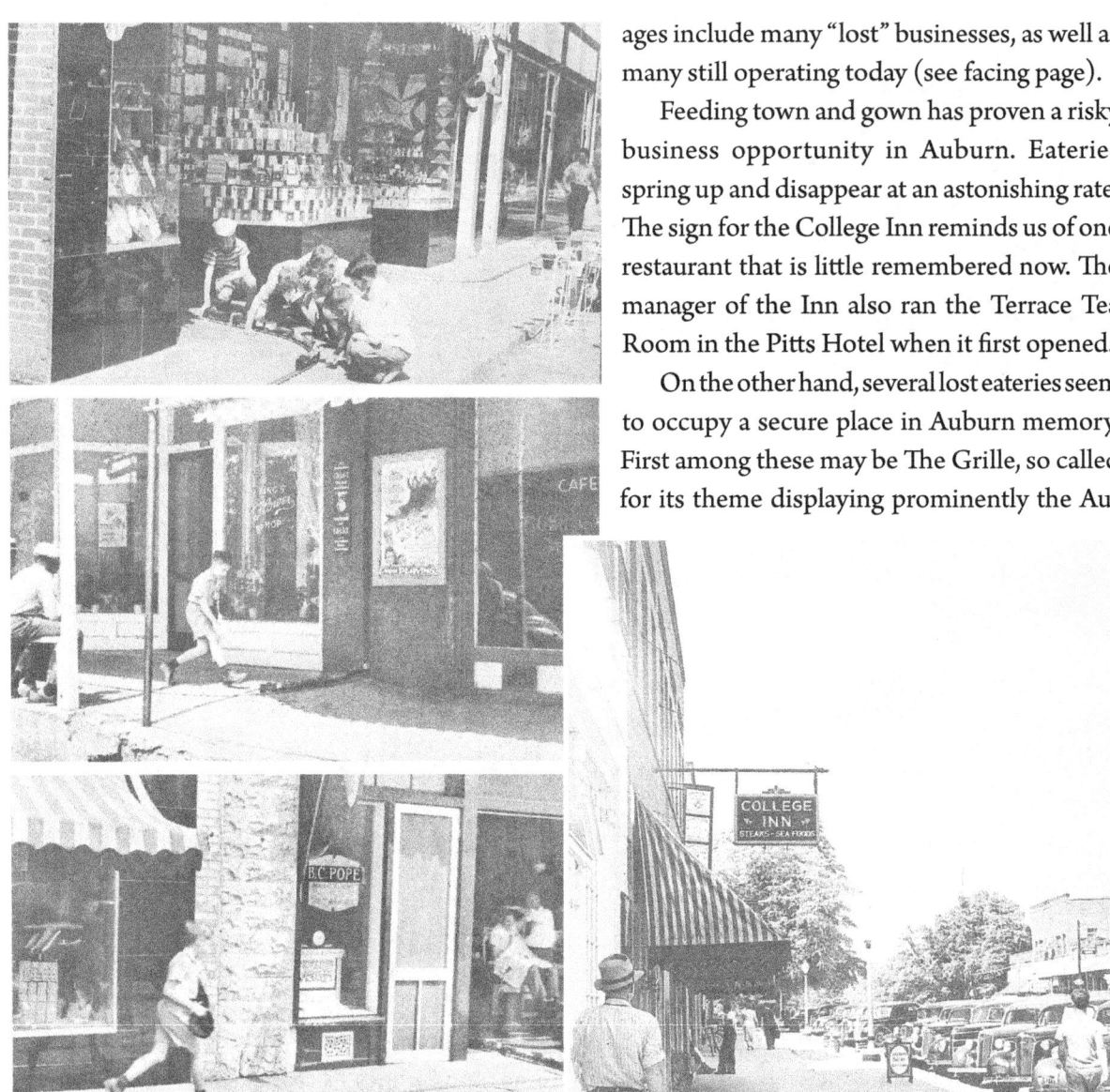

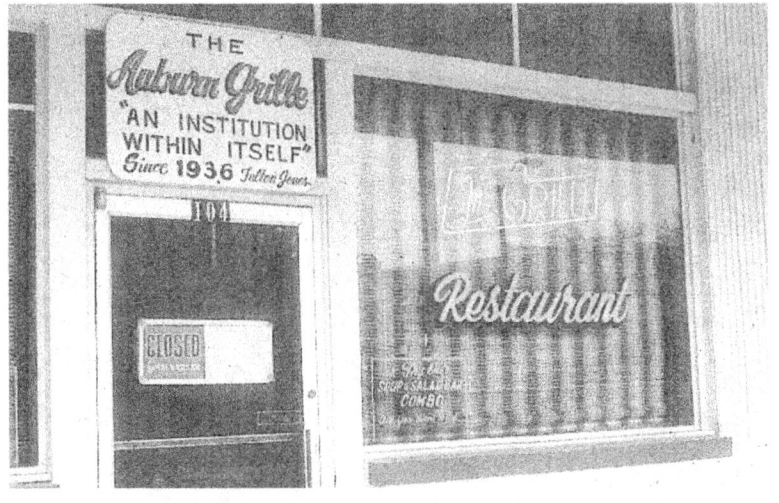

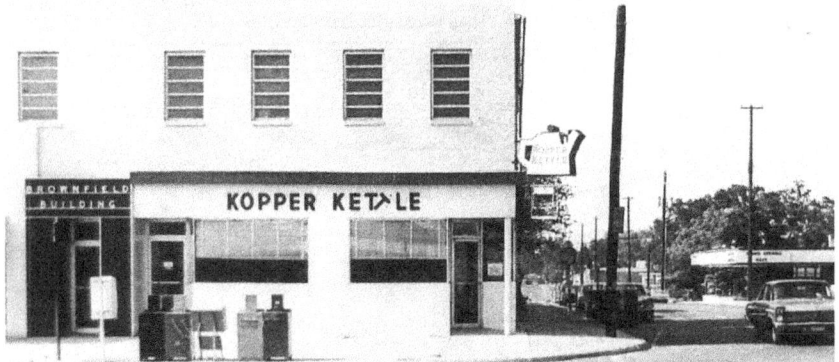

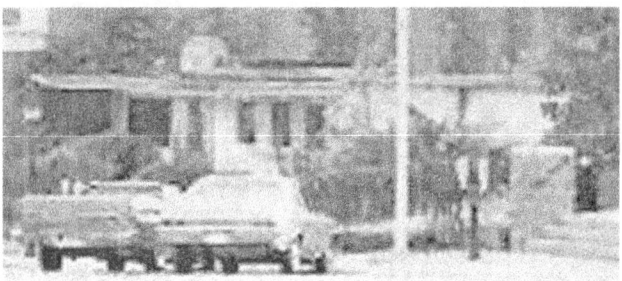

The Auburn Grille, Kopper Kettle, Roy's Diner